A TALL ORDER

by

KAPIL PATHARE

Popular Prakashan

www.popularprakashan.com

Published by Harsha Bhatkal
for Popular Prakashan Pvt. Ltd.
301, Mahalaxmi Chambers
22, Bhulabhai Desai Road
Mumbai 400026
www.popularprakashan.com

First Published 2016

(4447)
ISBN 978-81-7991-888-3

Cover Design: Evolve Multiventures LLP
Typesetting: Anjali Sawant

Printed by
by Repro India Ltd.
Navi Mumbai

Dedication

This book is dedicated to my beloved father, Jaykumar Khanderao Pathare for his unwavering support and encouragement.

Contents

Foreword

It took me only a short while to understand that Kapil Pathare not only understands the technical aspects of cricket, but equally important, has the passion and the knowledge that goes into the making of a champion. It is this heart that shines through in this book.

Kapil throws light on the life and times on some of my Indian contemporaries. I had battled them on the field for close to two decades. Even then, some of the insights in the book have been an eye-opener. With a wide range of back stories across various chapters, it was a delight to read this book.

Kapil not only shares stories about India's favourite cricketers, but also goes through the process that made them legends. This will surely inspire future generations of cricketers, not just from India but from across the world.

– Sanath Jayasuriya

Preface

Indian cricket has always been about great individual performers, but never about a great team except for a brief period in the 1970s and 1980s. However, it all changed with the advent of the generation of the 1990s.

These cricketers came together, provided stability in different ways, but results were still far from satisfactory.

First off the blocks was the Little Master Sachin Tendulkar who outlived, outplayed and outperformed all his peers. Then came the troika of Sourav Ganguly, Rahul Dravid and VVS Laxman in the same year of 1996. Together this quartet would form what came to be known as Fab Four of Indian cricket. This was truly the best-ever assembled batting line-up. Each had a different quality. Ganguly was feisty, Dravid was all steel, Laxman was an artist and above them all, was Tendulkar who was masterly in his approach.

Anil Kumble had probably the most unheralded start to any cricketer's career. Kumble was making the most of his ability, toiling away without any support at around the same time.

This group, however, needed some more worthy performers to make it a generation to remember. Starting off with the entry of Turbanator Harbhajan Singh, Indian cricket turned a corner. Then they all came one by one, the swashbuckling Virender Sehwag, the princely Yuvraj Singh, the pacy Zaheer Khan and the coolest of them all, Mahendra Singh Dhoni.

When you look at each of these individuals there can be no doubt that this was a fascinating era for Indian cricket, which led to the concept of this book. There was no debate on the choice of these 10 cricketers, for they made headlines, brought in new fans and made cricket a sport to fall in love with.

Together let's relive, relish and enjoy their performances yet again.

***

Acknowledgements

My father, Jaykumar Khanderao Pathare was born in Kolhapur and qualified as an electronics engineer before he moved to Kalyan on the outskirts of Mumbai to work with the Maharashtra State Electricity Board (MSEB) in 1959. He never returned to Kolhapur.

He established the Maxwell Electric Company, an electronics contracting firm, in partnership with his friend. In 1970, he entered the hosiery business with the VIP company. People affectionately referred to him as 'A True VIP'.

My father was a self-made man who had to shoulder the responsibility of the house at a very young age. Despite a very busy life, he would always find time to play cricket both in Kolhapur and later in Mumbai as well. Not many know that he was a state-level wicket-keeper and dreamt of finding a place in the Indian cricket team.

Sadly, he is not amongst us to witness the launch of this book about cricketers he admired so much. He would have been happy to see this book, since we spent a lot of time together discussing the achievements of these 10 extraordinary cricketers.

This book pays tribute to my father in a way that he would have liked the best. Hopefully, I have done full justice to the memory of my father with this offering.

I also want to thank my mother for making me what I am today.

My profound gratitude to Ashwini, my wife and partner in everything. My daughter Avyukta who I hope will realise the depth of my love for cricket when she grows up and reads this book.

A big thank you to Sunil, my elder brother and to Heena, Kanishk, Vandana, Aashish Shete, Karan, and Mayank who have always been an inspiration.

Thanks are also due to my dear friends Shantanu Samak and Chandresh Narayanan for helping me compile this book.

Thanks to all my relatives, friends and company staff for their support.

***

Sachin Tendulkar

Just as the 1980s were drawing to a close, a 16-year-old cricketer was making waves on Mumbai's maidans. With the arrival of Sachin Tendulkar, India now had a batting superstar capable of drawing crowds wherever he played.

Before Tendulkar came on the scene, the Mumbai batting school had produced the likes of Vijay Merchant, Sunil Gavaskar, Dilip Vengsarkar and Ravi Shastri who were now considered old school. They would bat all day long and play cautiously to save the side from possible defeat. However, not one of them was an entertainer who could wow the world. The advent of Tendulkar changed all that. From the time he started playing first-class cricket, he was setting standards for future generations to follow.

For those of us who were in our teens in the 1980s and the 1990s, it was almost as if we were growing up with Tendulkar as he scaled peaks rarely reached by an Indian cricketer or any Indian sportsperson for that matter.

A nation driven to despair by abysmal sporting standards, finally had something to cheer about. If there was one man or name that was synonymous with India at the time, it was Tendulkar. To make matters more interesting, Tendulkar started off his career in Pakistan, in what was the mother of all battles. It requires nerves of steel to pick a 16-year-old to take on the best in the world and that too in Pakistan. However, Raj Singh Dungarpur, the chairman of the selection committee, picked the youngster over a battle-scarred veteran Mohinder Amarnath.

So the baton was passed. I remember watching Tendulkar's debut series in Pakistan. The way he batted fearlessly even at that raw age was simply breath-taking. He was prepared to take risks. He was aggressive yet correct in his approach. The Pakistani fast bowlers Wasim Akram and Waqar Younis tested him severely, but he was prepared to fight fire with fire. There were a number of senior players in the Indian squad who were being pushed around. They were more restrained while playing against Pakistan, very unlike when playing other sides. Tendulkar was made of a different mettle. He took on Pakistan's best bet Abdul Qadir in what was a festival match.

In the Test matches too, Tendulkar was one of the key reasons why India came away unhurt despite predictions by most experts that they would lose 0-4. This was the start of something new for India. The 1990s were all about Sachin Tendulkar's blossoming into a world-class cricketer. His boyish looks also garnered a lot of interest wherever he travelled with the Indian squad, including New Zealand and England. When he missed out on his debut Test hundred in New Zealand in 1990, an entire nation wept with him. That was the impact he had on our psyche. Similarly, when he got his first Test hundred in England later in 1990, we all celebrated with him.

In Australia, in 1991–92 where India had assembled a cast of veterans including Vengsarkar, Shastri and Srikkanth, there was just one man who came away with his reputation absolutely intact, infact enhanced. Tendulkar had battled them on his own terms. The Aussies thought they could rattle this 17-year-old with pace and bounce, but it was just the challenge this teenage sensation loved. Watching him smash the Aussie bowling and puncture their exuberance on the fast Perth pitch was memorable. The entire dressing room would have realised that day that this young boy was going far.

In the 1980s, as youngsters we were fixated on whether Gavaskar would break Don Bradman's record of 29 Test hundreds. With Tendulkar, we realised that we had to set the bar much higher. This was again evident when India toured South Africa for the first time later in 1992.

The story was repeated. Only one man stood out — Tendulkar — he had just turned 18. He took on a whole new set of fast bowlers, on a fresh set of fast pitches. Tendulkar's reputation grew by leaps and bounds. So by the time Tendulkar arrived to play only his second Test at home in 1992–93, in the four years since his debut, he had a reputation to live up to. Tendulkar did not disappoint. He showed his countrymen why he was being showered with accolades the world over. Imagine such a scenario in today's India. Would we ever have our Indian cricket team play outside for close to four years without being seen at home?

Those were certainly different times.

Tendulkar was by now the most followed teenager that we had. We had not had a cricketer evoking this kind of interest ever. We had the likes of Kapil Dev and Sunil Gavaskar, but no one who could rival a Diego Maradona, a Pelé, or a Michael Jordan.

It was not just Tendulkar the batsman who got our love. We even fell in love with his bowling, especially in the Hero Cup semi-final in 1993 against South Africa. Jumping up and shouting in joy was something every Indian, including me, performed multiple times that cold November night. We were truly in the Tendulkar era. A number of world class, veteran players made their way out. Tendulkar's peers suffered loss of form and fell out of favour, but the man himself grew further in stature.

His reputation even gave fresh impetus to an old-fashioned English county side, Yorkshire, in terms of crowd support. Tendulkar was after all their first-ever overseas professional in 1992.

His rivalry was now with his contemporaries the world over. He started battle first with West Indies' Brian Lara. Then there was cricket's finest leg-break bowler, Shane Warne. Together, the trio defined the world of cricket in the 1990s. However, Tendulkar lasted longer than either of them.

He was by now becoming the one-man army battling for India against the rest of the world. He topped the batting charts in the 1996 World Cup and later that year took up the mantle of captaincy, too. But he realised very soon, like the rest of us Indians that he was only as good a captain as his team. Unfortunately, his side let him down at most times muffing up opportunities to raise his stature further.

India was becoming adept at snatching defeat from the jaws of victory! There was again a sense of despondency, which was lifted only when Tendulkar was relieved from the cares of captaincy. He was now a free bird and back to entertaining us in the best possible way. He took on his old nemesis Warne in what is now regarded as one of the best counter-attacks in cricketing history at home and in Sharjah in 1998.

Later at the 1999 World Cup when he had to leave the tournament mid-way to attend his father's funeral, an entire country mourned with him. That hundred against Kenya in the World Cup after re-joining the team is still an emotional moment. We were dependent entirely on the magic of one man. The burden of captaincy was back on his shoulders, but it was not the same Tendulkar.

The spark for some reason was missing and this time, it looked like Tendulkar was not comfortable with the crown. After a string of losses, he happily let go of the captaincy to become the batsman that we all had grown up to love. He entered a fresh phase in his career where he was one of the five senior players re-sculpting the Indian cricket team. Finally, it seemed like Tendulkar found colleagues who were on the same wavelength. Though no longer in an official leadership role, Tendulkar did require to be one of the men to be working in the background. With a number of young players debuting or making a mark at the same time, Tendulkar was revelling in his new position.

He was not yet a veteran, but a senior who was guiding the fortunes of an entire nation.

So it was hardly a surprise that Tendulkar was the one who stepped forward when the 2003 World Cup campaign got off on the wrong note. He first appealed to the nation to maintain calm and then raised the pitch himself with outstanding batting. Even though India ended on the losing side in the final, for Tendulkar this was a big step up in a career that was already star-studded.

Over the next few years, Tendulkar moved from being a senior player to a veteran cricketer. With the changing roles came a spate of injuries: his foot, then his finger, elbow and shoulder. After recovery, he came back refreshed to take charge yet again of the batting line-up. Changes in leadership did not affect his approach, because he was the one constant in the playing XIs. That said a lot about his ability to adapt to varying situations. He started with an earlier era, settled into his generation and then moved forward effortlessly with the next set of cricketers.

India started winning abroad with a new set of players who could battle the world. It was no longer just about Tendulkar, but that did not mean we did not care about him.

Tendulkar's own obsession was for India to win the World Cup in his final appearance in the mega competition (in 2011). He continued to scale peaks in the Test arena with records that are known by every cricket-loving Indian. He was now entering a crucial phase in his career where he wanted to achieve his dream of being part of a World Cup-winning team.

Even at that late stage in his career he managed to create magic. It seemed like he had unlocked a treasure house. To manage two hundreds against England and South Africa was a super start. He kept the fire burning for India and was the one reason why India did so well in the tournament. The best moment came in the semi-final against Pakistan at Mohali. I remember watching him get many reprieves thanks to dropped catches and technology. He deserved every bit of the luck that came his way. Life came a full circle for Tendulkar as he had scored every time the arch-rivals, at this mega event, had met since the 1992 World Cup.

In the final, the enormity of the occasion got to the Indian fielders and the bowlers. Even the chase seemed to be unnerving because Tendulkar left early, but thereafter the generation next of Indian cricket took over and managed to achieve what had been elusive since 1983!

For Tendulkar it was a moment to rejoice and reflect as the entire squad carried him on their shoulders around the Wankhede Stadium. The sight of him walking around the Wankhede Stadium as the crowd clapped for them is one I will never ever forget. I bet there wasn't a dry eye in the stadium that day. I think Virat Kohli summed it up well when he said that it was but a small token of appreciation for all that the master batsman had done for the sake of Indian cricket.

Speculation ensued about whether Tendulkar was retiring from cricket completely that night, or just from ODI cricket. Unsolicited advice poured from all corners, especially from the likes of Imran Khan. Thankfully, Tendulkar carried on. The only surviving members of his era, Rahul Dravid and VVS Laxman too hung up their boots leaving Tendulkar as the only link between not just his era, but the one after that and the one from the 1980s. He was now the elder statesman in the midst of a number of cricketers who were born when he started battling Wasim and Waqar. That was the longevity of the man!

His fans were now obsessed with one milestone: about him reaching the unique mark of scoring 100 international centuries. It was a long wait for all of us as we prayed long and hard for him. I cannot think of any Indian cricket fan who has not had a special prayer of his or her own to help Tendulkar reach a new high! It was hardly surprising that Tendulkar's quest for his 100th international century became a national passion. It took almost a year to move from 99 to 100, but that was also because India was going through a transitional phase with a number of youngsters coming in. When he finally achieved the landmark, Tendulkar celebrated in his habitual understated way.

To be at the Wankhede Stadium and hear the chants of 'Saaaachin Saaaachin!' was a thrilling experience. To be part of a crowd singing the national anthem and see the little master on the screen was out of this world. The entire stadium would fall silent if he got out. This showed the impact the man had on the psyche of an entire nation.

When he retired from both forms of the game, it was heart-breaking for me. I was on an international business tour when I heard the news of him retiring from ODI cricket in late 2012. Then in 2013 when there were reports of him retiring from Tests too, I had a few sleepless nights. It was difficult for all of us who belonged to his generation to imagine a cricket team without Sachin.

Finally, came the official announcement that Tendulkar was retiring. We spent the next couple of months reliving the Tendulkar years. Finally, the moment arrived. India did a quick demolition job of West Indies. Tendulkar himself walked off with tears in his eyes and then he came back to leave an entire nation in tears with his farewell speech. We stood in silence and clapped each time he spoke that day at the Wankhede Stadium. It was an emotional moment for all of us. I cannot think of a higher accolade for Tendulkar than the full house that turned up to see his final game at his beloved Wankhede Stadium.

The sight of him waving goodbye for one final time and the Indian team giving him a guard of honour was one to behold. This was happening even as his contemporaries Dravid, Ganguly and VVS Laxman were near the boundary line applauding.

Thanks a lot for the memories Sachin and pardon the few who booed or those who called it 'Endulkar'!

Stories like yours can never end, they live forever in the memories and hearts of a cricket-loving nation.

***

Anil Kumble

"It ain't about how hard ya hit. It's about how hard you can get it and keep moving forward. How much you can take and keep moving forward. That's how winning is done!"

– Sylvester Stallone as Rocky Balboa

This could well be a description of Anil Kumble. Before he became the third-highest wicket-taker in the history of Test cricket and a legend, Kumble was a common man. He did not have the benefits of two of his equally great contemporaries — Shane Warne and Muttiah Muralitharan. The list of Kumble's faults was long. He did not spin his leg-breaks as much as Warne, the leg-spin master. He did not float the ball above the eye line of batsmen, trademark of a conventional spinner. Whenever he took wickets, critics diluted his effort pointing to the home advantage and the tailor-made pitches.

It was a common refrain. For the first decade of his career, Kumble toiled without getting accolades, but he never complained. He might have opened up with some close friends, but did not let the bitterness affect his game. He kept working on his strengths as a cricketer. Eventually, the naysayers fell silent as Kumble chugged along merrily, filling the wicket column regularly at home and abroad. Though he was a spinner, Kumble was aggressive in his approach, never giving anything away to batsmen.

He loathed batsmen taking a boundary off him. Those iron-melting stares he gave to fielders who erred spoke volumes about his mind-set as a bowler. You could not find a more avid or tenacious competitor on the field than Kumble. Studying Kumble's career as a cricketer offers valuable tips about survival instincts and the art of keeping your head high even on your toughest day.

However, that is just one aspect of Kumble. He was an equally caring team-mate, popular among players for his professional approach and attitude. For long, he had been their 'Anil bhai.' When the effort was set in motion to create a players' association in line with the one in Australia or England, Kumble was at the forefront. Players' welfare had always been a top priority for Kumble. His popularity among the players was evident when they invited Kumble to the dressing room to be part of the celebrations, after winning the 2011 50-over World Cup at the Wankhede Stadium in Mumbai.

Kumble did not snap his ties with cricket post retirement. Unlike many former cricketers, Kumble did not restrict himself to coaching or commentating. But his involvement touched several areas — administration, running a player management firm, offering expert/technical inputs on the game to the International Cricket Council (ICC) and the Board of Control for Cricket in India (BCCI), using his stature as a cricketer to run wildlife campaigns, etc. Seldom has a cricketer had a presence in so many areas of the game after bidding adieu. Kumble could well be India's first Sportscrat. It is a great lesson in keeping yourself relevant and not merely resting on one's laurels.

Of course, Kumble will be remembered long for his exploits on the field. Let us take a closer look at some of his efforts.

1. **6/12 v West Indies, Kolkata:** This was a teaser. The performance in the Hero Cup 1993 final against the West

Indies offered glimpses of the bowler Kumble would go on to become in the future. West Indies was still a considerable power in world cricket then. They had some fine players like Brian Lara, Richie Richardson, Carl Hooper and Phil Simmons in their ranks. Chasing 221 would not have been a big task for them, but the Caribbeans ran into a rampant Kumble. Their middle and lower order did not stand a chance against the accuracy and bounce that Kumble generated from the Eden deck.

"It was a fine spell and I will cherish it fondly because it earned India a fine victory in a tournament final," Kumble said later.

More than the victory, the spell showed Kumble's ability to rise to a big occasion. Opponent, conditions, nature of the pitch, nothing mattered to him. Those who need a lesson in grabbing the bull by the horns need not look beyond that 6/12 of Kumble.

2. **Kumble v England at Home, 1992–93:** Pitch was made for Indian spinners and English batsmen were not particularly good against tweakers. But none could have imagined the misery England had to face against Indian spinners, especially Kumble, who pocketed 21 wickets from three Tests. England batsmen did not find a single way to counter Kumble. His pace and bounce were just too much for them to handle. Richard Blakey, the wicketkeeper, would never forget that tour as Kumble destroyed his confidence on his first overseas tour.

   Detractors may not give too much weight to that effort against England, a combination of old players nearing their sell-by date and youngsters unaware of the deep pits of international cricket. However, Kumble did not choose the England team. Sensing an opportunity and cashing in on it are two entirely different skills. Kumble had both.

3. **10 Wickets against Pakistan, Delhi, 1998–1999:** It was a wonderful solo performance. One bowler against 11 opposition batsmen. Kumble won each of those little battles. It is all the more praiseworthy because the feat came against Pakistan, as adept as anyone in playing spin. It all came together for Kumble on that day at the Ferozeshah Kotla.

   The effort took Kumble to cricketing immortality. Javagal Srinath bowled wide of the off-stump so that he would not take a wicket even accidentally. When the moment came his way, Laxman held on to a catch offered by Wasim Akram, Kumble's 10th wicket. Teamwork can achieve the impossible. Kumble and the Indian team underscored that point on that day at the Kotla.

4. **3/93 and 4/66 v England at Leeds, 2002:** The Headingley Test against England in 2002 will primarily be remembered as a match of the Indian batsmen. After all, they had piled up 628/8 declared, a total constructed on hundreds by Rahul Dravid, Sachin Tendulkar and Sourav Ganguly and a gritty 68 by Sanjay Bangar. But India then needed bowlers to chip in to complete the job. Kumble picked up three wickets in the first innings, including that of Mark Butcher, a batsman who can pitch a tent in the middle.

   In the second innings, Kumble took four and added the big scalps of Nasser Hussain and Alec Stewart. The 7/159 might not look as rosy as some of Kumble's other figures. But it came at a time when critics pointed out his away record. The performance, perhaps, marked Kumble's turnaround from a domestic titan to an all-terrain bowler.

5. **24 Wickets against Australia in 2003–04:** Kumble, perhaps, would not have got many chances in that Test series but for a finger injury suffered by Harbhajan Singh. How he exploited that opportunity! Tendulkar, Dravid, Laxman, Ajit Agarkar, all had their champagne moments on that tour. But the real hero was Kumble. His bowling kept Australia on their toes all the time. His intensity never flagged even once in all the three Test matches he played. It was like a relentless hunter chasing its prey.

   In cricketing terms, it was one of the finest efforts by Kumble overseas. In fact, one of the finest by an Indian bowler away from home. There were many candidates such as Jason Gillespie, Zaheer Khan, Brett Lee and Stuart MacGill for the bowling honours. But Kumble surpassed them all by light years.

6. **Wounded Hero, 2002:** Lionheart. Kumble could only be termed that for his gritty effort at Antigua against the West Indies in 2002. Mervyn Dillon hit Kumble square on the jaw, and he spat out blood. But he batted for a further 20 minutes. In normal course, that would have been the end of Kumble's tour, because a surgery was prescribed. But Kumble was cut from a different cloth. Taking a backward step was unknown to him. People stared at him with disbelief when he came out to bowl.

   He did not just turn his arm over, but bowled 14 consecutive, intense overs, besides taking the wicket of Brian Lara. What could have prompted him to come out when the safer option was to sit in the dressing room and take the earliest flight to Bangalore?

"I just did not want to sit around doing nothing," he said later. The reply might have seemed self-effacing, but we cannot miss the underlying passion for the game and his desire to contribute to the team even while injured.

7. **Hundred at Oval, 2007:** It was a magic moment. India had Dravid, Tendulkar, Ganguly, Laxman and MS Dhoni but the least fancied man got India's lone Test hundred on that England tour in 2007. It came at the Oval. Kumble had always been more than a handy batsman, especially in the longest version. Even men with few batting skills had posted a Test hundred. And Kumble's moment came in his 36th year and after 118 Tests. He speared a Kevin Pietersen delivery through the gap between stumper Matt Prior's legs, and lifted the bat in joy to celebrate a special moment. The entire dressing room and the Oval crowd were on their feet to applaud a popular hero.

   Later he said: "I raised the bat because I did not want Steve Bucknor to signal a bye. The ball had brushed my bat and I did not want him to make a mistake."

   In that match, it helped India reach 664 in their first innings, ensuring that the visitors would cling on to a 1-0 lead and win the Test series in Old Blighty after a gap of two decades. The Kumble hundred is a sparkling example of perseverance and burning desire to achieve an elusive goal.

8. **Kumble the Captain and the Tour of Australia, 2007–08:** Many felt that Kumble should have been given the reins of the Indian team much earlier because of his man management skills and inspirational abilities, besides being an awesome performer himself. The chance finally came in 2007 after Dravid stepped down from the hot seat

after the tour of England. Soon, Kumble was confronted with a crisis, massive enough even to disrupt the bilateral ties between India and Australia. In the acrimonious Sydney Test, which Australia eventually won, Indians accused Bucknor of sub-standard and biased umpiring. Later it snowballed into an issue of ethics as the Indians openly expressed their displeasure at some Australian tactics on the field.

Kumble stated: "Only one team is playing in the spirit of the game, and you know who it is."

After the Test, Indians did not board their scheduled flight to Perth, venue of the next Test, and stayed back in Sydney. They wanted umpire Bucknor to be kept away from the rest of the series. Then there was also the racial abuse allegation against Harbhajan Singh to be sorted out. It was a huge moment even for Kumble, then a veteran of 17 years in international cricket. But he handled those controversial and delicate times deftly, keeping the team together and ensuring that emotions did not boil over.

Once the dust settled, India reached Perth with a lingering sense of injustice. Kumble ensured that his teammates channelised their pent-up anger in the right direction. The result was a win for India at Perth, one of the toughest venues for a visiting team. Kumble played the role of a diplomat and a leader of men with aplomb.

9. **Kumble and IPL:** The Indian Premier League (IPL) was born towards the fag end of Kumble's career. By that time, Kumble was in the late 30s and had already decided that he would not appear for India in ODI and T20 internationals. However, he joined the IPL, an arena presumed to be fit only

for youngsters. But the old warrior left an impression here too. In the 2009 edition of the IPL held in South Africa, Kumble, then playing for Royal Challengers Bangalore (RCB), emerged as the second highest wicket-taker. It was an inspiring sight to see some veteran cricketers like Kumble, Warne and Tendulkar competing with younger players, and often outplaying them. It was an indication of Kumble's desire to defy the odds, and therein lies a message for us to keep working hard to achieve our goals. Age is just a number, and what matters is effort.

10. **Kumble, the Administrator:** Post retirement, Kumble stepped into cricket administration by becoming the president of the Karnataka State Cricket Association (KSCA). As it happens with any new administrator, there were a few wrong notes during his tenure too. He succeeded in refurbishing M Chinnaswamy Stadium into a modern venue, besides continuing to offer his vast wisdom to BCCI in his capacity as the Technical Committee chairman.

    But the striking point of his administrative stint was the eagerness to make cricket the centre point of the association. It is a message for administrators in other walks of life. Ensure transparency and work with a dedicated mind.

These examples are just token instances from the career of an extraordinary cricketer. His contribution to Indian cricket and the sport in general could never be measured fully. Of course, he will be remembered forever as the biggest match-winning bowler India has ever produced. The 956 wickets he took in Tests and one-day internationals combined prove the point.

His finest contribution is the fighting spirit he displayed throughout his career and the courage he showed to overcome his limitations stand as beacons for millions of young cricketers. He underlined that point during his final press conference in 2008 at Delhi.

"I had to go through a lot in the early part of my career. People questioned my ability, my fitness, my form, my bowling and the effectiveness of my bowling."

Despite such constant criticism in the early part of his career, Kumble stayed brave and ended up in the pantheon of legends.

Anil Kumble has always been a fighter, ready to take on any challenge. Post-retirement, he has stayed in character. He applied for yet another challenging assignment — that of head coach of the Indian team — a position he was appointed to in June 2016.

***

Sourav Ganguly

He was the one man the whole world loved to hate, but when it came to delivering for Indian cricket, he was always at the forefront. He was ridiculed and mocked, but Sourav Ganguly managed to pull together a career of note!

I remember Sourav from his early days when he won the Ranji Trophy with Bengal in 1990. He shot to national fame with his performances for Bengal. He was consistent and the Indian selectors were looking for a medium-pacer and all-rounder. India already had rich resources in Kapil Dev and Manoj Prabhakar as all-rounders. Ganguly was meant to add value on that infamous 1991–92 Australia tour.

Ganguly's tryst with destiny started on a sour note. He spent close to four months carrying drinks and gloves, and also ended up alienating the officialdom apparently because he behaved like a prima donna or so they said! He played one ODI against West Indies, struggled to get going and thereafter was forgotten. Ganguly's tales did the rounds and the cricketing world assumed that he was gone for good.

He had gone back to the rigours of domestic cricket. The closest he came to playing an international match was when he was chosen for a Board President's XI one-day game at Delhi against the touring England side. He came into bat at number three even as current TV star Navjot Singh Sidhu was smashing the ball all over the Kotla. That innings was the turning point in Sidhu's career, but Ganguly is most remembered for being hit on the unmentionables!

Then we had the concept of India 'A' sides. Ganguly was almost ritually a part of these sides. Not many of us in India followed the contests and it would usually be dismissed in a nondescript news item in newspapers. It was hardly a foreteller of the future.

The low phase in Ganguly's career coincided with India's dream run at home between 1993–95. All the ills that came to the fore on overseas tours were forgotten as India were merciless at home. It was a phase when India did not look at more youngsters. So the likes of Ganguly, Rahul Dravid and VVS Laxman did the rounds of the selection matches but never played any grade above that.

India's disastrous campaign in the 1996 World Cup meant that the selectors were looking for fresh blood. There were a number of names being bandied about, but Ganguly was way down the order. The problem was that he was still being viewed from the prism of the 1991–92 Australia tour where stories of him behaving like a prima donna had circulated. It was hardly a surprise that the likes of Dravid and Vikram Rathour stole a march over him.

Ganguly's name first came up during a match in Sharjah when former India opener Arun Lal was asked on air by Harsha Bhogle about selections for the upcoming tour of England. Arun Lal was the only one to take Ganguly's name and he was immediately mocked by Bhogle.

It turned out that Arun Lal was not the only one to get a negative reaction on Ganguly's selection. The national selectors too received similar reactions. It was one of the most controversial selections in recent times. For the first half of the tour to England, India chose four spinners and just three new ball bowlers. Ganguly was controversially chosen as the fourth new ball bowler and an all-rounder. When chairman of selectors Gundappa Viswanath was asked about it, he hardly appeared convincing about the choices his panel had made.

When the scrutiny of the names had been done, Ganguly's name stood out. The BCCI secretary at the time, Jagmohan Dalmiya was also the convenor of the selection panel. All sorts of insinuations about Dalmiya's influence started doing the rounds. Even before he boarded the flight, Ganguly was alleged to have been a quota candidate. There was not much that Ganguly himself could do. Everyone was going to have to wait because the selectors had named the squad and that was the end of it.

For Ganguly that tour was the biggest test. His first time out with the Indian squad and that too after four long years was a big moment in his career. I remember seeing him play Sussex in one of the many tour games. He appeared elegant and confident about himself. Ganguly's approach was a typical left-hander's. In India, we had only seen southpaws, in those days, such as WV Raman and Vinod Kambli before Ganguly. So to discover an elegant left-hander à la David Gower was a dream come true. However, Ganguly's presence in the playing XI was still not a certainty!

Fate had other ideas. Two senior players, Sanjay Manjrekar and Navjot Sidhu were dumped for the final ODI on that England tour. India was forced to pick Ganguly and Dravid. Ganguly played an attractive knock and everyone marked him as the player to watch. Later, Sidhu packed up and went home in controversial circumstances, opening up spots in the side.

But that was not enough to get the tour selectors to push his case. India lost the first Test at Edgbaston and there were calls for wholesale changes. India responded in kind, handing debuts to Ganguly and Dravid.

Ganguly shone with the ball, but his biggest litmus test was his Test debut as a batsman on the hallowed turf of Lord's. He surpassed all expectations and the rest, as they say, is history. The English took to his elegant batting and started describing it like a poem. The moment that Ganguly achieved his maiden Test hundred on debut, all the abuses and insinuations hurled at him by everyone were forgotten. He was embraced as one of India's favourite sons. He then followed it up with another hundred in the final Test. India had found someone who almost equalled the efforts of their skipper Mohammad Azharuddin, who had scored hundreds in his first three Tests.

What an end to an England tour which started with a lot of despair, but finished on a high note! This was the start of the new phase in Indian cricket with a number of young players starting off, who would end up becoming legends.

From his debut tour onwards, Ganguly became a regular in the team. A change in leadership meant that Ganguly had more responsibility. He was given bigger roles like opening in one-day cricket with Sachin Tendulkar. He was already batting at number three position in the Test matches.

The home season of 1996–97 did not see him raise the bar as far as his performances were concerned, but he was by now one of the most loved Indian cricketers. The fans looked up to him and considered him to be a match-winner. His bowling was a big plus.

On the tours of South Africa and the West Indies, Ganguly's performance in Tests was nothing to write home about. He was even dropped for one of the Tests in the West Indies, but he stole the show in the one-day matches.

He became a darling of Indian fans when he single-handedly defeated Pakistan at Toronto in a set of ODIs that were played for three years. His all-round show meant that Pakistan were routed 4–1 for the first time in history. Pakistan captain Ramiz Raja had to hang up his boots thanks to Ganguly's brilliance.

Amazingly, after all his exploits, Ganguly was still not in top form in India. He finally struck gold in the 1997–98 season against Sri Lanka and Australia.

Ganguly's biggest moment thereafter came in England during the 1999 World Cup. In conditions that helped the seamers, Ganguly was more than a handful as a bowler. Then he was top notch with the bat as he blasted Sri Lanka in the company of who else but Dravid. His knock of 183 was spoken of in high terms by critics and fans alike. Ganguly's effort remains one of the most talked about in the history of Cricket World Cups. It is hardly a surprise that for fans Ganguly was their 'Dada' or big brother!

India's World Cup ended in disaster, so another leadership change followed. Azhar and Tendulkar were involved in a game of musical chairs. But there was one series in Toronto, this time against West Indies which did not have Tendulkar.

Ganguly was the one chosen to lead and he impressed everyone with his aggression. He was involved, led from the front and was generally animated. For an India that had only seen a Javed Miandad do something similar, it was quite a pleasant surprise.

A disastrous Australia tour and the controversy surrounding Azhar, meant that Ganguly was thrust into the captaincy. (Tendulkar had had enough of his tryst with captaincy and decided to not touch it again.) Ganguly was immediately seen as a messiah of Indian cricket. Unfortunately, Ganguly's first full series in charge was controversial. It turned out that his opposite number Hansie Cronje and some other key South African players had taken money to underperform. That put a blot on a famous series win for India.

Then the match-fixing scandal blew up in everyone's faces. It consumed Azhar and Ajay Jadeja. That forced a change of approach with a number of young players being drafted in. Ganguly was now given a free hand.

In came a new generation of Indian cricketers who were hungry, confident and aggressive. Virender Sehwag, Yuvraj Singh, Zaheer Khan, Harbhajan Singh and Ashish Nehra were talents of note.

India needed this fresh blood urgently and the presence of a young captain meant that this transition happened seamlessly. Whether it was the 2000 Champions Trophy where Zaheer yorked his way to stardom or the home series against Zimbabwe, this was a new India on view.

Then Ganguly also had the company of India's first foreign coach, John Wright. He was unstoppable on the field and away from it. He had a perfect set of seniors to back him, especially with vice-captain Dravid. Ganguly could not have asked for more unqualified support from his seniors, a rare occurrence in Indian cricket.

It was the historic series against Australia in 2000–01 which really shaped Ganguly's leadership. The turnaround and the remarkable series win were down to Ganguly's leadership. His choices, VVS Laxman and Harbhajan came good, giving Ganguly and the Indian team a fresh lease of life.

But for these individual examples of brilliance, Ganguly's time as Indian captain would have ended. He gave a glimpse of the coming years with his leadership. The reputation of the sport had been battered and bruised by the allegations of match-fixing. The Indian public needed someone who would help them regain trust and interest in the sport that they all loved so much.

Ganguly seemed the answer to their prayers. He was so involved and aggressive that Indian cricket never felt the same again. Finally, for the Indian cricket fan, Ganguly gave them a side that they could be proud of. Ganguly, however came close to losing his captaincy a few times, especially in the 2001–02 season. His senior players suffered a rash of injuries, especially Tendulkar, Javagal Srinath and Laxman, thereby putting a lot of pressure on the rest of the squad. However, that phase proved to be a learning curve for Ganguly and his young side. They came out with some credit.

After just one series in South Africa that season, pressure started building on Ganguly, but India gave a good account of themselves at home in 2001–02 against England.

Then India registered their first Test win in the West Indies since 1976, under Ganguly at the Port of Spain in 2002. It was a moment to savour. The performances were outstanding and the presence of an all-round bowling attack with plenty of choices was a first in Indian cricket history.

But this euphoria did not last long as India lost that series to West Indies and Ganguly was left a broken man at the end of it all. A golden chance had been blown away. India's next trip in 2002 was to England. India's famous win in the tri-series with Ganguly waving his shirt is now part of cricketing folklore. The more important win came at Headingley. India battered England with the bat and then stung them with spin in overcast weather.

It was hardly a surprise then that India had begun its new era in cricket with wins overseas in Test matches. That was the stated aim of Ganguly and Dravid. They wanted to go around the world, win and establish a legacy that no one could match.

India did that more often under Ganguly's leadership over the next two–three years, winning in Australia and of course, in Pakistan, too.

The only place where India did not do anything of note was in New Zealand where it became difficult to differentiate between the outfield and the pitch. In terrible batting conditions, India struggled but surprisingly even New Zealand found it difficult. Ganguly came under pressure yet again, but because India is an ODI obsessed nation, the onset of the 2003 World Cup did not see any change in leadership.

India started the 2003 World Cup slowly but finally gained miles only to lose in the final. Ganguly himself scored three hundreds in the tournament to end as one of the leading lights. Unfortunately, Ganguly's hold over the squad was slowly starting to slip away. He made some controversial choices which would come back to bite him.

First, his time in Australia with the legendary Greg Chappell was going to prove controversial. Ganguly came away convinced that Chappell had to be the one to coach India! Then his own fights with the leadership in the BCCI came to the fore. He controversially left the side stranded on the morning of a Test at Nagpur against Australia citing injury.

One could sense from the body language this was no longer the side that he so famously sculpted. He was banned for slow over rate. The change of leadership from Ganguly to Dravid was done in a hurry. Again, Ganguly was forgotten by one and all.

This was a sign of things to come with a number of changes slated to happen in Indian cricket. Ganguly had managed to get Chappell installed as a coach. Everything seemed to be going to plan for Ganguly. It appeared that Indian cricket was going into a new era with Ganguly still in charge, but it was not to be.

Ganguly had a fallout with Chappell because the former Australian captain wanted the skipper to stand down from the playing XI. Ganguly and Chappell had a serious fight in Zimbabwe and all hell broke loose. Finally, the BCCI had to step in to do some firefighting. Ganguly was dumped as captain, Chappell got the total backing of the powers that be and Indian cricket was not the same again.

Ganguly slowly started slipping below the radar. India would pick him and then not play him like they did in Pakistan, when he supplied drinks as a reserve batsman! Then for about nine months, Indian cricket forgot about Ganguly. Every selection committee meeting ended with the Ganguly question. Dravid was ready for the Ganguly question at every press conference and Chappell almost always avoided the query.

India started off well sans Ganguly, especially in the ODIs, but then slipped away, especially against the better sides like Australia. So much was the impact of the Ganguly axing that it angered Bengal. There was an ODI at the Eden Gardens against South Africa in 2005–06 where the visitors were cheered. Dravid and his side was constantly booed and the whole experience left a bad taste in everyone's mouth.

Ganguly's axing found an echo in the parliament, with the BCCI president Sharad Pawar, a government minister, being asked by his colleagues to change his decision. Finally, after a series of poor performances in ODI cricket and a disastrous first half of a South Africa tour in 2006–07, India was forced to recall Ganguly.

It was a photo op to cherish, when Ganguly shook hands with Chappell in South Africa. No one expected Ganguly to make an impact immediately, but he did! His knocks coupled with the brilliance of the fast bowlers, especially Sreesanth, gave India their first Test win on South African soil.

The fact that India went on to lose the Test series hurt a bit, but Ganguly made a tremendous comeback. He was even back in the ODI side and was named man of the series in the series against Sri Lanka!

Then at the 2007 World Cup, India lost to Bangladesh and all blame was pinned on Ganguly's approach while batting. Everyone felt he slowed down and some even called it selfish. Ganguly had become such a divisive figure that he inspired comments from both sides!

India was dumped from the World Cup of 2007 and the players became villains. Chappell was ousted and Ganguly heaved a huge sigh of relief. The England tour that followed underscored Ganguly's utility especially as a bowler. He provided crucial breakthroughs which helped India win their first series in England in 21 years.

Ganguly was keen to continue playing all formats. He was especially keen to play the inaugural World Twenty20. But he reluctantly agreed to step aside from the T20 squad along with Tendulkar and Dravid. Indian cricket changed track yet again under a bright young man like Mahendra Singh Dhoni. Things were not the same again for Indian cricket.

Finally, Ganguly lost his place in the ODI squad for good to a younger man. The Bengal man was hardly impressed and made his displeasure known to one and all.

His performance in the Test format took a beating. The only saving grace was a 'Man of the Match' showing on an absolute dust bowl at Kanpur in what was Dhoni's first Test as captain. Ganguly appeared to have lost the plot in the series away against Sri Lanka. India was undone by the controversial Umpire Decision Review System (UDRS) and the magical Sri Lankan spinner Ajantha Mendis. Ganguly was immediately dropped from the series that followed against Australia.

A change in the selection panel with Dilip Vengsarkar being replaced by Krishnamachari Srikkanth meant that Ganguly was brought back. It was a typical lame start to a pre-Test press conference by Ganguly. He spoke in general terms about the series. Then came the stunning announcement that he was retiring!

He took everyone by surprise, but that was his style. He did well in his final Test series scoring a hundred.

In his final Test at Nagpur, the new captain in charge Dhoni gave him an opportunity to lead the side in the dying moments of the match. It was a tremendous sight to see Ganguly in charge for one last time and was a grand gesture by Dhoni.

Ganguly played for three more years in domestic cricket and IPL. He continued to be a divisive figure even then. Ganguly had a run-in with another Australian coach, John Buchanan this time over him being stripped of captaincy at

Kolkata Knight Riders (KKR). So much so that KKR even offloaded Ganguly from the franchise. Kolkata was again up in arms and Ganguly was at the centre of it all.

Then Ganguly moved base to Pune Warriors, but things were not the same again. Indian cricket's man of change finally bid adieu to the game and moved into the commentary box. Here too he was frank, upfront and aggressive in his approach.

It was this attitude which marked the Ganguly years. Today's Indian cricket is a legacy of the Ganguly era which will live on forever.

Now he is making an impact as an administrator, leading the way as the Cricket Association of Bengal (CAB) president.

***

Rahul Dravid

It was way back in March 1992, when I switched on the television to see a day-night match in India.

It was a rarity in those days to see coloured clothing in India, but that was one odd day with Hyderabad's Lal Bahadur Stadium switching on the lights.

This was the first time a day-night match, featuring an Indian representative side, was being played outside the multipurpose Jawaharlal Nehru Stadium in New Delhi. There were a few upcoming players who caught my eye that day.

New Zealand had the likes of Stephen Fleming and India too had a few future stars in their midst. But there was one man who stood out in the pack. This man was someone who would turn out to be an all-time great for India, Rahul Dravid. Ironically, it was Dravid who was also the India captain for that under-19 series.

While the younger Indians were battling New Zealand in colour, around the same time the senior team was involved Down Under in the first colourful Cricket World Cup in 1992. That Indian team of the 1992 Cricket World Cup too, had a teenager, a certain Sachin Ramesh Tendulkar. Little did Tendulkar or Dravid know that they would soon team up and become a memorable pair.

Dravid meanwhile continued to slog in domestic cricket. He was being considered for India 'A' trips.

Dravid toiled in domestic cricket and continued to impress as he made more runs. Indian cricket it seems was still not ready for the right-handed Karnataka batsman.

India continued to do well in home-like conditions as they played a lot of cricket at home, Sri Lanka, Sharjah, even as they squeezed in a short tour to New Zealand. Indian cricket changed personnel only in 1994, when all-rounders Manoj Prabhakar and Kapil Dev were rested for the Australasia Cup in Sharjah.

This was going to be a moving year in many ways for Indian cricket. The baton was going to be passed. Long-serving vice-captain to various Indian captains, Ravi Shastri, hung his boots as he could no longer put up with the strain to his knee. Shastri had been a forgotten man for Indian cricket since December 1992, when his knee injury put him out for close to eight months.

Then by the time the 1994–95 Indian home season started, the greatest cricketer India produced at that stage, Kapil, was showing signs of slowing down. It was disastrous at times to watch a hero just limbering up and bowling at military medium-pace. The final nail was the spell in Faridabad, in 1994–95 when the visiting West Indies side went on a rampage. Kapil then suffered an injury, forcing him to be out of the rest of the ODI bilateral series and of course the first-ever triangular series in India, Wills World Series. This World Series was meant to be run on the lines of the annual World Series Cup matches that happened in Australia then. The fact is that the tournament ran for close to five more years till 1998–99.

Kapil missed out on playing the second ODI in that bilateral series against West Indies at Bombay, which was being staged as a benefit for his long-time teammate Dilip Vengsarkar.

The year 1994 had been euphoric for Kapil as he had scaled the Mount 431 peak, that seemed insurmountable at one stage. This peak was the Sir Richard Hadlee record for most Test wickets in history. Kapil had inched to 400 on the 1991–92 tour to Australia. But then Kapil slowed down due to importance placed on spinners.

As the 1994–95 season wore on, Kapil realised his injury will not recover and announced his retirement. That was a big void to fill. Then came another unsavoury incident which started the whole doubt around match-fixing in Indian cricket. Prabhakar and wicket-keeper Nayan Mongia were batting together in the Wills World Series contest at Kanpur against West Indies. India had sealed their place in the final at Kolkata, but they still needed to win to maintain the winning momentum.

Mysteriously, Mongia and Prabhakar slowed down, hurting India's cause to thereby hand West Indies a win on a platter. Indian team management was furious, the selectors led by GR Viswanath swung into action and made a couple of changes. Prabhakar and Mongia were out, in came Vijay Yadav (after a year) and Dravid!

With Chetan Sharma already in as Kapil's replacement, there was really room for just one of the two new faces, which had to be spunky Yadav, as he was the designated keeper. Dravid watched as India went on a rampage against New Zealand in the final league match at Delhi and then in the final, West Indies had no answer for the second successive year at the Eden Gardens.

It all seems like a blur now, but yes Dravid did make the Indian team first in 1994, and that too because of someone else's misdemeanour. India celebrated the second successive title triumph at the Eden Gardens. Everything was forgotten thereafter. The circus moved to Vizag where the kits did not arrive on time to resume the bilateral series. Also changed was the attire of the two sides, as whites replaced coloured clothing. Prabhakar and Mongia returned, Dravid and Yadav were cast aside. Yadav never even came close to representing India, Dravid went back to the grind of proving himself all over again.

That 1994–95 was quite a moving season as the concept of 'A' team cricket started in India. An England 'A' side led by Mark Ramprakash made its way to India for a three-Test series. Dravid started showing signs of what India might have in their midst in the years to come.

The season of 1995–96 was a season of hope for India. Dravid started off playing against the touring New Zealand side in a side game and then came close to a World Cup selection. But it was not until the World Cup ended in disaster for India, that Dravid's fortunes rose. The fact that Karnataka won the Ranji Trophy in that 1995-96 season helped matters.

Dravid had earned his international debut in Singapore! He played one more tourney in Sharjah, but did not set the world on fire. It was felt by all that with a few forced changes following the sudden exit of Prabhakar and the end of the first phase of Vinod Kambli's career, there was room for new faces.

The next target was the England tour. There were a lot of permutations and combinations in play, but there was one constant factor, the presence of Dravid. The English tour itself was dramatic in the way Dravid and Sourav Ganguly made it to the XI, first in the ODIs and then Tests.

The fact that Navjot Sidhu, another senior cricketer, walked out of the tour in a huff helped matters. The whole process hastened the arrival of the generation next in Indian batting. Dravid and Ganguly grabbed the opportunity with both hands.

The most enduring memory of the 1996 England tour was a disconsolate Dravid walking away from the Lord's ground. His knock of 95 meant that he missed the chance to score a debut ton. He followed that up with another top-class knock in the third and final Test at Trent Bridge.

With Sidhu under a ban, Prabhakar retired and Kambli out of favour, there were more youngsters on their way. It therefore made sense for the selectors to hand the captaincy to Tendulkar. He set about building his own side. Dravid, Ganguly and to some extent VVS Laxman were going to be the cornerstone of his plan.

Dravid was still not batting at number three for India in Tests and he struggled a bit to get going in the ODIs. The home tri-series featuring Australia and South Africa, underlined these problems. The number three was reserved then for Ganguly with Dravid batting at six. India romped home in style against Australia in a one-off Test, claimed the tri-series title and then beat South Africa too.

Dravid did not have a big role to play in all of this. But with eight Tests in South Africa and West Indies, there was bound to be some work for the young right-hander. I still remember distinctly watching the complete surrender at Durban in the return series. To see just one man, Dravid, stand up to the South African pace confirmed what I had always believed about him.

Dravid was the man India needed up the order to counter and blunt the South African pace attack. He was pushed up the order to number three, finally. It paid dividends almost immediately with Dravid getting his first Test ton at

Johannesburg. It was here that India came close to registering their first away Test win, outside the subcontinent, since 1986. India, however, achieved a win at Johannesburg 10 years later under Dravid's captaincy.

But the rain gods and the tardy ground staff at Wanderers had other ideas. The next abiding memory of Dravid was in the final of the tri-series that followed the Test matches. The way Dravid took on South Africa in the rain-hit final, was a sight to behold. His six off Allan Donald elicited abuse from the White Lightning, but the Karnataka man was unmoved. He almost steered India to a title win in South Africa, but it was not to be.

It seemed like Dravid would always be the bridesmaid, but never the bride. He showed flashes of his quality on the West Indies tour that followed. That series was another missed opportunity as India failed to hunt down a modest target of 120 at Barbados to register a famous series win in the Caribbean.

Dravid then showed yet again why he was a top-class batsman, when he allied with Ganguly in a run chase at St Vincent. As long as Ganguly and Dravid were at the crease, the chase was in sight, but the moment they departed, India collapsed and missed out yet again!

The 1997–98 season could have seen Dravid grow in stature, but he was stymied by the lack of support from the selectors. They dropped him from the ODI team saying he could not play the format. This led to a furore, because India was still warming to the concept of specialist squads like we have now. Dravid received a lot of support, but he was nowhere close to being considered for the ODI squad.

It was not until the New Zealand tour of 1998–99 that Dravid found his way back into the ODI squad. Even then, it was only because he had scored hundreds in each innings of the Hamilton Test. Thereafter, there was no stopping him as he went from strength to strength. For the ODI squad, Dravid worked hard with former Australia coach Bob Simpson, who was with the Indian team as a consultant. Simpson taught him the importance of rotating the strike in ODI cricket.

It paid dividends and we had yet another Ganguly-Dravid jugalbandi, this time during the 1999 World Cup. During the 1998–99 season at home, Dravid had issues with the touring Pakistani side's varied attack led by the magnificent Wasim Akram. Dravid found Akram and his band of strike bowlers difficult to handle, but he gained vital experience.

It was during the 1999 World Cup that he struck two brilliant hundreds, the first against Sri Lanka. Then against Kenya, he lit up the Bristol ground. It was here that Dravid was handed the role of a wicket-keeper for India in the ODI format.

Following another World Cup disaster, there was another change of guard. Tendulkar reluctantly took the hot seat again. For Dravid another season of mishaps awaited. His best moment came at Hyderabad against New Zealand when he teamed up with Tendulkar yet again in an ODI for a top-class hundred. That apart, the season of 1999–2000 will be remembered for Dravid's struggles in Australia. He did not grow as a batsman.

And in the new millennium when there was a change of guard again with Ganguly taking over as captain, Dravid's role also underwent a change. He was now among a group of seniors. He was Ganguly's second-in-command and was meant to be the brains of this core group.

Dravid and Ganguly together set about changing the mind-set of the Indian cricket establishment. It was their diligent approach that gave India its first foreign coach in John Wright. Dravid particularly pushed for Wright because he realised while playing for the English county side Kent (Wright was the coach there at the time in 2000) that India needed something more to reach the next level. Together with Ganguly, Dravid shared the dream to take Indian cricket to a new high.

India set about restructuring the squad and its work ethic. Not many know that it was Dravid who did all the hard work in terms of strategising and planning while Ganguly led on the field. Dravid was the ideal deputy to Ganguly, with Wright also playing a huge part. Ganguly also received great support from other seniors like Tendulkar, Anil Kumble and Javagal Srinath. India's crowning moment of 2000–01 was winning the Test series against an invincible Australia at home. Dravid played a huge part in the revival of fortunes, not least of all because of his mammoth 180 and his breath-taking stand with Laxman at the Eden Gardens. He was even prepared to do the verbals for a change to take on Australia captain Steve Waugh.

This was also a phase when Dravid grew as a batsman. He was now the undisputed number three batsman for India in Tests both at home and away. The biggest purple patch in his career came in 2002–04.

He scored hundreds everywhere, in the West Indies, England, Australia and Pakistan. It is no coincidence that Dravid's purple patch as a batsman coincided with India's rise as a credible Test team away from home. His blue riband moment was the series in England in 2002. It was on this tour that Dravid reached the next level. It was also during this phase that Dravid kept wickets to lengthen the batting in ODIs. This worked wonders because India started doing well in the limited-overs format with Dravid contributing with the bat and gloves.

India's World Cup journey in 2003 may have ended in disaster in the final, but the campaign was a happy one thanks mainly to Dravid keeping wickets and helping the cause. Going on the Australia tour in 2003–04, Dravid was the undisputed number one Test batsman in the Indian squad. He had even led India once in a Test in that season when Ganguly was rested following an injury.

The 2003–04 Australia tour, especially the match-winning knock in Adelaide and the famous alliance with Laxman was the highlight of the tour for me. Later in the season however, seeing Dravid fined for allegedly tampering with the ball during an ODI tri-series match spoilt it for me.

Later in Pakistan in 2004 on a tour that happened almost at the last minute, his knock in the deciding Test at Rawalpindi was worth its weight in gold. He scored 270, his highest in Tests and sealed a famous series win for India, their first in Pakistan. But that tour will always be remembered for Dravid pulling the plug on Tendulkar's possible double hundred at Multan. It led to some bad blood between the two, but it was not long before it was all sorted out.

Dravid had taken the first steps towards captaincy of India's cricket squad. Ganguly was losing grip of the side. Dravid had to step in a few times during the 2004–05 season and this indicated that a change was in the offing.

This was also the time India began its search for the next coach. This time again the focus was on a foreigner. Dravid along with other seniors was keen on former Aussie all-rounder Tom Moody getting the role. Ganguly was solely focussed on former Australian captain Greg Chappell being appointed. That proved to be fatal, Ganguly lost the trust battle with

Chappell, and he lost his place in the side for a year. Dravid immediately took over and led India on a winning streak chasing totals in ODIs. He gained further respect when he was named in a World XI to take on the-then world champion Australia.

Later in 2005–06, Dravid played a big part in a partnership that almost broke the record for the highest opening stand in Test history, against Pakistan. That Virender Sehwag and Dravid fell just three short was heart-breaking, but it made up for the disappointment that followed in the same Test series.

India's best moment came in West Indies, when Dravid completed 10 years in international cricket and faced a lot of backlash for the Ganguly exit. Dravid hung on, led India to a Test series win in West Indies, our first there since 1971. His knock in the deciding Jamaica Test has to be amongst the best he has played and amongst the best I have ever seen.

However, India's ODI form dipped, the public started losing faith and there was an outcry. So back came Ganguly, as Dravid led India to their first-ever Test win in South Africa. The World Cup that followed was an utter disaster.

Quite often, Dravid's legacy as a captain is viewed purely from the ODI standpoint and not from the Test prism where he achieved a lot in his tenure. India's early exit from the World Cup caused a lot of heartburn. Dravid was expected to resign or be sacked. Instead the blame fell on just one man, Chappell, thereby ending an ugly chapter.

Dravid was still leading India and again he achieved something rare, a Test series win in England, for the first time since 1986. India's achievements were clouded by the lack of a push for a win in the final Test. But Dravid had achieved what Azhar and Ganguly had failed to do, win a series in England.

The debate around the first-ever World Twenty20 and the possible make-up of the squad was happening during the same tour. MS Dhoni was the new chosen one, because Dravid along with the seniors opted to sit out.

It was only later that Dravid announced his resignation as captain even as Indian cricket welcomed its new baby, the Indian Premier League (IPL) on the same day. The loss of captaincy meant that a dry spell with the bat followed. It even led to Dravid being dropped, yet again, from the ODI squad. He was now struggling with the bat in Tests too. He did play a small part in India's first Test win at Perth in 2007–08 though.

Just as Kumble and Ganguly retired in 2008–09, pressure on Dravid increased too. The dry spell continued, but the selectors developed amnesia yet again as they recalled Dravid to the ODI squad in 2009, primarily because of a few injuries. Dravid regained form in Tests but the ODI dream was over.

Dravid was losing control of his destiny it seemed when he was pushed down the order, when newbie Cheteshwar Pujara was pushed to number three in the 2010–11 series against Australia.

Dravid sat at home and watched India win the 2011 World Cup. But that gave little indication of how he was preparing for his final stretch in international cricket. He scored hundreds in West Indies and England in that final season of 2011–12. His match-winning hundred in West Indies was the only one which came in a winning cause, away from home. His valiant knocks in England did nothing to stem the damage that India suffered to its pride as they capitulated 0-4. Dravid's show meant that he was back in the ODI and T20I squad. However, he quit both the formats at the end of the series.

It was then onto the final tour of Dravid's international career, to Australia. This was yet another disaster, as India were whitewashed 0-4. Dravid kept getting clean bowled and it was a sad sight to see that happening. That was the biggest indication of an era ending.

When the dust settled on the tour and India moved away from its obsession of the limited-overs format, Dravid called time on his international career in his own understated way. We will never know whether his hand was forced or he decided to move on his own.

But we did know his next few years would be in the role of moulding his IPL side, Rajasthan Royals. Here too, Dravid was let down by his teammates. For a cricketer who led a principled life in his career, this was the moment which tore him apart, as he saw his teammates being charged for spot-fixing.

I have since tracked Dravid's life as a coach of the India 'A' and India under-19 sides. He has brought a sense of calm and discipline to a bunch of hopefuls. There can be no bigger teacher than the best Test batsman India has ever produced. He was and will always be 'The Wall', the man who brought calmness to the dressing room.

***

VVS Laxman

This is a story told to me by a journalist friend of mine. Back in the summer of 2003, a junior reporter waited near the staircase leading to the dressing room of the M Chinnaswamy Stadium. His wait was for VVS Laxman. Laxman was then the hottest property in Indian cricket after that epic 281 against Australia at Kolkata. The reporter was certain of Laxman's reply even before making the interview request. After all, why would the creator of one of the most magical Test innings speak to a reporter not known to him?

Eventually, Laxman, dragging a kit, approached the staircase landing after a workout at the National Cricket Academy (NCA). The request was made hesitantly. The expected denial and the anticipated arrogance and the feared explosion did not happen.

Instead came the query, "What's the interview based on?"

The question was steeped in politeness, accompanied by a warm smile and handshake. It was his first interaction with Laxman. He could have just walked away without even looking at him. He could have easily denied the interview request. But he chose to respond differently. It was a lesson in humility. It just rubbished that old theory: "Nice guys do not finish first."

Those who know Laxman from his early days in Hyderabad say the right-handed batsman had always been an epitome of humility. They even say it is a peculiarity of the city. They reel off several examples — Tiger Pataudi, M L Jaisimha, Venkatpathy

Raju, Mohammad Azharuddin and those countless players who play for the city in domestic cricket.

In the years that followed, we had the good fortune to see Laxman at various places from New Delhi to Adelaide — on and off the field. By that time, Laxman's stature in Indian cricket had touched new heights. He had become an integral part of that sparkling batting club featuring Sachin Tendulkar, Rahul Dravid, Sourav Ganguly and Virender Sehwag. Laxman tormented bowlers around the world, sometimes like an artist and some other times like an artisan.

Only his batting style changed to suit the occasion. Laxman's personality remained fixed. Many times, I wondered how Laxman kept his composure despite handling a difficult job as a batsman. Often he was asked to bat lower down the order — mostly at number six — and marshalled the lower-order batsmen around him. Many times, his innings was the difference between a good day and bad day for India in the park, sometimes between victory and defeat itself. Once a journalist asked him in an interview as to how he felt doing the job of a firefighter time and again.

"Aren't you tired tackling the pressure situations? Don't you like to go up and bat with a little more freedom?"

His reply was: "For the team, I will do this another thousand times."

No further explanation was needed. Many of Laxman's knocks too carried the traits of his personality — positive and competitive without being over the top.

Let us take a closer look at some of his efforts.

1. **167 v Australia, Sydney, 1999–2000:** This was the time when Laxman opened the innings. India had their backs

to the wall in that Test against the rampant Aussies, and were facing a deficit of 402 runs in their second innings. The outcome of the Test match was a foregone conclusion once India was bundled out for 150 in their first innings. But India at least needed to put up a semblance of a fight. Laxman took up that task. He cracked 167 off 198 balls with 27 sweetly hit fours. That innings was one for the connoisseurs, the kind you need to enjoy taking the match situation out of your mind. It was a curtain-raiser to many other Laxman innings that left the Aussies scratching their chins in frustration.

2. **281 v Australia, Kolkata, 2000–01:** The innings will forever remain the 'greatest'. Runs were never piled up faster and in bigger numbers, than Laxman's stylish 281 at the Eden Gardens. But few other knocks could match his in terms of defying the gravity of the situation. Laxman was up against a team that had stitched together 17 Test wins in a row. He had to negate the finest bowler of all time, Warne, and another set of quality bowlers, who loved to be at the throat of the batsmen. Of course, he also had to keep his focus away from the Aussies' 'friendly banter'. His knock was a distillation of mental strength and focus against an in-your-face opponent. When it was over, the Aussies were drained, they didn't have anything left to offer and timidly accepted the defeat. Laxman's knock was a lesson in swimming against the tide.

3. **148 and 32 v Australia, Adelaide, 2003–04:** They were two different knocks, played in two different situations. The 148 was played as a second fiddle to Rahul Dravid's masterly 233. On occasions, Laxman brought out his wizardry, sinewy wrists uncoiling to send the ball to the

fence. But the innings was more about supporting Dravid and Laxman, himself capable of sparkling stroke-making, eschewed his natural instincts and did just that. It was a lesson in finding happiness in your partner's success.

The 32 was just as important. Chasing 230, India was in a mini-turmoil at 170 for four after the fall of Sourav Ganguly. Aussies might have hoped to take a couple more quick wickets to reach India's tail. India needed someone to take a few quick runs and close the gap with the target. Laxman took up that job. A 34-ball 32 followed with six wristy boundaries. It released the pressure on Dravid too.

Laxman was not there in the middle when India registered a famous and rare win Down Under. But that hardly mattered. That 32 was a fantastic example of selflessness and also one of setting aside personal goals for the team.

4. **69 v Australia, Mumbai, 2004–05:** It was not the Laxman one expected on that day at the Wankhede. He came down from Mount Olympus to play a more commonplace knock. It was the trailer of one of those mini-classics which Laxman would go on to play in the latter part of his career. Australia had already bagged the series. Now, they wanted to rub salt into India's wounds with a 3-0 series win. They were well on course for it, dismissing India for 104 in the first innings and then building a 99-run lead. So, India needed a better effort in the second innings to have some chance to stay in the Test.

   The old warhorses Sachin Tendulkar and Laxman, who was promoted to No 3, milked 91 runs and then another pair of old boys — Dravid and Laxman — added 48. Laxman was never really fluent despite hitting 12 fours.

Often he was clay-footed. But he never let his guard down and fought as much and as long as he could. His readiness to come out of his comfort zone is also a life lesson.

5. **103 Not Out v Sri Lanka, P Sara Oval, Colombo, 2010:** Again, this was no magical Laxman. The P Sara Oval was no colourful stage in wonderland either. In that boiling cauldron, India were chasing a tough target in the fourth innings and a win away from home. And those who followed Indian cricket would tell several stories about India's fragility in the fourth innings. The Hyderabadi braved a hurting back, a potent Lankan attack and the regular fall of wickets at the other end to lead India's victory march. No stumps were uprooted, no obscenities were hurled and no fists were pumped in anger. Laxman embraced that massive moment in a stately fashion.

   A champion batsman was at his grittiest best there. But more than the knock itself, the humility Laxman showed in that victory touched me. This is not to say that sportspersons should not be allowed to vent their emotions on the field. Characters have a space in sports. Sports definitely requires a John McEnroe or an Andre Agassi or an Eric Cantona. But sports also needs pillars of calm for keeping that fine balance. In that, Laxman belongs to the category of a Tendulkar or a Pete Sampras. In short, that innings taught us about the need for equanimity to be successful in life.

6. **73 Not Out v Australia at Mohali, 2010–11:** This innings showed why Laxman was indeed Very Very Special. As it was at the P Sara Oval, Colombo, here too, Laxman was struggling with a sore back and batted at No. 10 in the first innings. Once Aussie bowlers found

their radar, the target of 216 looked way out of India's reach, and at the fall of eighth wicket India still needed 92 runs. Just a matter of a few more overs, Ricky Ponting might have imagined. Laxman, the master persuader of lower-order batsman, first made Ishant Sharma stand with him to make 81 for the ninth wicket, and then cajoled and shouted at Pragyan Ojha to make the remaining 11 runs to seal one of the finest Test victories for India.

The innings could be compared to rowing in terms of overcoming the pain barrier. A rower needs to feign ignorance about his aching limbs to complete the race, often pushing the raft up the river. Steve Redgrave will tell volumes about that art. Yes, it is an art — overcoming the pain barrier. It takes courage to smile even when pain flows through your veins like hot ink from a tattoo needle. Laxman did that and more on that day at the PCA Stadium, educating us about the need to have that in-the-trenches resolve to achieve your aims. It also told us about lifting your partner/colleague to contribute to a big mission, helping him to tide over his limitations. It requires great mental courage, fortitude, vision and faith. Laxman's knock will be remembered as an example for that.

7. **96 v South Africa in Durban, 2010–11:** Laxman was at it again. A magnificent effort in the second innings. He made a match-winning 96 against the likes of Dale Steyn, Morne Morkel and Jacques Kallis on a tough pitch, where no batsman from either team managed to go past 40. Ashwell Prince's 39 not out was the second highest score in that Test. In cricketing terms, it proved to be the difference between the two sides. But a great performance

on the field is not just restricted to the realm of sport. It often carries a much deeper message and Laxman's innings was no exception. He just imposed his will to win on the South Africans. The message: if there is a challenge take it head on.

The last chapter of a wonderful career came fittingly against Australia in 2012. The magic had waned. Those wrists were no longer whipping the balls from off-stump to mid-wicket. His back and knees were finally giving in. Runs, once a torrent, had eased into a trickle. Laxman saw Australia, a rival whom he tormented relentlessly over a decade, stomping over his team for a 4-0 series win. But the inner turmoil was not on show. It was a perfect example of how to tackle a tough situation. Many times, we have seen players struggling to cope with a lean patch. For them, climbing down from a high is a painful experience, the ultimate embarrassment. Perhaps, he knew that there was no return for him to the cricket field. Here, Laxman went through it with dignity.

The aforementioned knocks were little sparkling shards that made Laxman a fine batsman and a role model for aspiring cricketers and for us in general. But there are some other less obvious factors as well that we tend to overlook in the splendour of Laxman's batsmanship.

For long, Laxman was a pure artist with the bat, finding impossible angles and gaps on the field with those supple and strong wrists. He carved knocks similar in perfection, precision and beauty to Michelangelo's frescos at the St Peter's. When Laxman was at the crease, batting was elevated to the sphere of high art. But even that sublime batsman could not wither that unstoppable force – time.

Gradually, injuries began to creep into his body. Back spasms curbed his movement, forcing him to adopt a crouched stance. Knees began to crumble away, affecting his running between the wickets. Of course, he was not the fastest but that dodgy knee made it all the tougher for him. Despite using a light bat, painting an innings like the old became increasingly difficult. He needed to change to survive longer in international cricket.

It was also a matter of ego. It might have been tough for Laxman to transform himself into a plebeian. But he went through the grind — for himself and for the team. The wizard went into hiding, but the team got a steelier match-winner in all conditions. Only a few like Tendulkar did it. In the latter part of his career, Tendulkar kept many of his shots like the hook in the locker room before entering the field. India benefitted by that changed approach. Others like Virender Sehwag and Viv Richards resisted the change. But it is tempting to think about the results if Sehwag and Richards had tweaked their game to suit their advancing years.

Laxman was large-hearted enough to trade the thrill factor in his game for efficiency. In another interview Laxman was asked as to how tough it was for him to adopt a different batting approach.

"You just need to realise what's good for you as a player, and periodically assess whether I have been contributing to the team's success. Depending on the answer, you need to change or persist with an approach. What matters is contributing to the team," he said.

This attitude has set apart Laxman and players of his tribe. It told us the importance of creating an awareness about the environment where you live and work.

Laxman had rarely put himself ahead of the team. He would have loved to bat at number three, the position of the play-maker. However, he went down the order without complaints to accommodate Dravid at one down. But once Laxman pressed his own case. He had never been an opener, but the team management made him open the innings quite a few times. It was not benefitting him and thereby the team in any way. Eventually, Laxman had to communicate through a press conference in Bangalore in 2000, that he no longer wanted to open the innings. It was a desperate call to the powers-that-be to grant him the wish.

It was not a vicious personal attack on selectors, team management or the captain, but a strong statement of intent nevertheless. Individuality has to be kept even in a team environment and Laxman showed that through his appeal.

Great players have not always found worldwide acceptance. Some may be popular in their own dressing room, but will be a failure in grabbing the respect of the opposition. There was no doubt of the greatness of the all-conquering Australian team of the 1990s or 2000s, but they seldom received the universal love that was showered on the West Indians.

In an individual contest, Laxman was popular among his own team members and among the rival teams. He maintained strong ties with Dravid, a companion from their days together in age-group cricket. Their days together in the Indian dressing room only deepened that relation, and it was not surprising to see the two players building some tall edifices of runs in each other's company – in Kolkata and in Adelaide to name some. Another close friend of Laxman in the dressing room was Zaheer Khan. A bond that started from sharing a hotel room during the famous Kolkata Test against Australia in 2001, only grew thick over the years.

Towards the end of his career, there was some gossip about his rift with the-then captain Mahendra Singh Dhoni, especially during the Test series Down Under in 2012. However, it was Dhoni who came on air during a Test match against New Zealand to pay tribute to Laxman. Stories remained just that — stories.

The third T20 international between India and South Africa at Kolkata in early October 2015, underlined the fact that Laxman's popularity in the Indian dressing room has not dimmed one bit.

The rain and wet outfield had delayed the start and the Indian players noticed Laxman's bird-printed shirt, soon they displayed a placard: "We Love Your Shirt Laxman Bhai". It was not just the love for the shirt, but for the man himself. In true Laxman style, he limited his reply to a polite, smile-accompanied "Thank you." Even the Aussies loved and respected one of their biggest tormentors of modern times along with Tendulkar and Brian Lara. The sight of an entire SCG crowd standing up to applaud him in 2000, revealed their reverence to an exceptional performer and an equally exceptional individual.

Laxman should not only be remembered for his exploits with the bat but also for the values he upheld on and off the field.

***

Harbhajan Singh

Harbhajan Singh was spotted by chance at a nets session of the Mumbai Ranji side in 1997 at Mohali. In fact, former Indian pacer Balwinder Singh Sandhu offered him a chance to play for Mumbai but an unsure Harbhajan turned it down. During that season, Harbhajan came to the notice of a lot of people.

The one man who noticed him most was former Indian opener Navjot Singh Sidhu. Now, Sidhu was a brilliant batsman against off-spin and had carted the likes of Muralitharan around grounds the world over. Even Sidhu was beaten by Harbhajan's skill.

I remember reading snatches about Harbhajan's early brilliance in newspapers. I was an avid follower of Ranji Trophy cricket and would follow the performances of some young cricketers.

Indian cricket was waiting for an effective spin bowler. Anil Kumble was there, but his spin partners kept changing. Left-arm spinners like Venkatapathy Raju, Sunil Joshi, Nilesh Kulkarni and Rahul Sanghvi had been given a go. Then there were off-spinners like Aashish Kapoor, Rajesh Chauhan and Noel David. However, India did not have an effective partner for Kumble.

The Indian attack was incomplete. I remember that tour by Australia in 1997–98, when India won the first two Tests in a canter at Chennai and Kolkata, but still, there was something missing.

It was apparent that in the bowling department, India needed fresh blood.

Lots of names were doing the rounds, but no one really spoke about Harbhajan at that stage. Harbhajan's start was something similar to that of a first-time entrepreneur.

We had not learnt or heard of the unconventional in our business or sport till then, especially not cricket. The most we had seen in terms of the unconventional was BS Chandrashekhar with his freak action or Krish Srikkanth with his maverick approach.

In business we had the story of Dhirubhai Ambani rising from rags to riches through sheer hard work. Harbhajan had something similar to achieve through his early years. When he was handed the ball at Bangalore all those years ago in 1998, I was reminded of the time my father handed me the responsibility of looking after one aspect of our business.

Harbhajan looked nervous, did not smile and was like a schoolboy amongst adults. After all at 17, that's what it is like for any young boy or girl. He had seniors like Sachin Tendulkar, Azharuddin, Sidhu, Sourav Ganguly, Anil Kumble, Javagal Srinath, Rahul Dravid among others around him. He had a lot to gain from being there. Despite being nervous he did not let that get in the way of a good performance.

For Harbhajan, the task was tougher because he was starting off on a clean slate. A weaker man would have given up, but not Harbhajan. He picked up an early wicket, that of Greg Blewett.

You could see what that wicket meant for Bhajji. He relaxed and claimed one more wicket, that of Darren Lehmann. Indian cricket fans and most certainly I felt that we had unearthed a gem.

I saw yet another glimpse of what Harbhajan was capable of when he snapped up another youngster Ricky Ponting. The two would go on to have countless battles in the future. But we got the first dekko at Sharjah in 1998. During one of those million tournaments there, Harbhajan foxed Ponting and then gave him a royal send-off. It looked ugly on television, but who cared! As an Indian cricket fan, I loved what I saw.

After all when was the last time you saw an Indian cricketer giving it back as good as he got? Kiran More and Manoj Prabhakar may have, but the list was pretty limited. We needed to have that killer instinct to make our presence felt, and Harbhajan gave us a first look of that. However, his career yo-yoed over the next couple of years. He was being replaced by the likes of Nikhil Chopra for one-day cricket and India's Test engagements reduced over the next couple of years.

India's bowling stocks were getting depleted, Srinath was selective about the matches he played. Kumble was affected by the workloads.

The other pace bowlers Venkatesh Prasad and Ajit Agarkar were still not ready to take over the mantle. Yet, though Harbhajan was touring with India's Test squads to New Zealand and then Australia, he never made his presence felt. He showed a total lack of confidence.

Slowly, Harbhajan slipped into the domestic circuit. It was at this time that he harboured hopes of moving to North America and working like many others from his state. An incident at the newly-started National Cricket Academy (NCA) in Bangalore left a bad taste. Harbhajan was asked to leave the camp early and we all felt that was the end of that!

But fate had other plans: he was still on the minds of new Indian captain Sourav Ganguly, but he had not shared his thoughts as yet. The selectors were trying to push for Harbhajan's statemate Sarandeep Singh, but Ganguly was fixated on the rangy Sardar.

I remember wondering at the time in 2000 about how a talented young man had been lost for good. There was something about Harbhajan that struck me as being interesting. He was in-your-face, aggressive and not a typical Indian who would not speak his mind in front of his seniors.

India's youngsters are taught to be respectful, not get back at their seniors and generally be yes-men at a younger age. Harbhajan changed that view for Indian youngsters. He taught them that you can be firm yet be respectful.

Thankfully, when Australia arrived in India in early 2001, Ganguly had not given up on his pet obsession: Harbhajan. He pushed the selectors to pick him for the squad that was to take on Australia in that historic Test series.

Harbhajan was like a number of start-up entrepreneurs who needed a visionary like Ganguly to back him. He took on the might of the Aussies and spun their doom!

I remember telling my friends that my belief in Harbhajan had come good.

India had found the missing link in their bowling armoury and a bespectacled Kumble had now found an able ally. So much so that Kumble gave up his spectacles for contact lenses! Harbhajan would not have been anything without the presence or impact of Ganguly in the second stage of his career. Overnight the Aussies coined the term 'Turbanator' for him.

Everyone loves a bad boy, but Harbhajan was not a bad boy. He was different, he did not follow the beaten path and liked to forge his own way to the destination.

Harbhajan had grown in stature by the end of 2001 and he continued to be in news with his performances. He scripted many famous wins especially in England in seaming conditions in Headingley in 2002, alongside Kumble. He made an impact even in ODIs and Tests at home. But the big moment came in the 2003 World Cup, when alongside the Galacticos of Indian cricket he turned around a fledgling campaign. Harbhajan was among the many Young Turks who had now made it to the Indian squads in both Tests and ODIs.

All these youngsters had one leader, Ganguly and they followed him like he was a Pied Piper. Ganguly backed all of them and his most trusted weapon was Harbhajan. But old doubts about Harbhajan's action came to the fore again. He was pulled back a bit from bowling, but he fought this like only he can.

Indian cricket was going through the process of another churning and this time in terms of leadership. Harbhajan was a Ganguly protégé and made no bones about it. Harbhajan was the sort who needed backing and support from his captain. He was not someone who could perform irrespective of the change of leader. If anything, that was a failing in him. There came a time when Ganguly was replaced by Dravid as captain, Harbhajan was not the same force. Yes, he did pick up wickets, but it was not the same as before. There was another important change that impacted Harbhajan and that was the arrival of Australia's great batsman Greg Chappell as a coach.

This was the time when Harbhajan revealed his combative side the most. He took on Chappell, openly disagreed with him over the dropping of Ganguly. Above all, Harbhajan was willing to challenge Chappell. This was unheard of even in the hard-nosed Australian culture. Both sides were at fault in my view.

Harbhajan showed scant regard, Chappell also showed an utter lack of understanding of the Indian psyche.

Harbhajan felt he owed respect, but Chappell showed none and vice-versa. Harbhajan and the others were rated as cancer by Chappell. This created further bad blood in the camp. Matters came to a head on the 2006 West Indies tour, when Dravid, along with Chappell, had issues to settle with Harbhajan. When the offie finally played in the deciding Test at Jamaica, you could see what the match meant for Harbhajan. His celebrations after taking wickets, indicated that there was something amiss in the Indian camp. Harbhajan was undoubtedly at the centre of it all. He was alone at times because most of his peers like Zaheer Khan, Ganguly were out of the reckoning. The others like Ashish Nehra had been forgotten. There was just Yuvraj Singh to give him company. This was a changed Indian squad and Harbhajan took time to adjust to the changed scenario. His performances dipped. India went from good to bad, to worse, in ODI cricket in 2006–07 and the culmination of it all was at the 2007 World Cup.

India was knocked out early, a public enquiry followed and Harbhajan was dropped yet again by the selectors. It was felt that this was it, Harbhajan was forgotten again, but he made a dramatic comeback at the World Twenty20 in 2007. He made an instant impact, and it was almost as if he had almost never lost it. There were a couple of massive changes in the Indian squad.

Dravid had quit captaincy and Chappell had opted out or had been pushed. So this was the start of a new era under new captain MS Dhoni who was almost Harbhajan's age, but started off seven years later! Then there was another important change in that Harbhajan had his long-term spin partner Kumble as the Test captain.

These positive changes meant that Harbhajan reclaimed his career after it seemed like it had been lost yet again. This quality of Harbhajan, in which he came back from the brink, made me his unabashed fan. But controversy and Harbhajan were never too far apart. Just as I rediscovered my fandom for Harbhajan, came his infamous Monkeygate spat with Australia's Andrew Symonds.

Harbhajan was ready to give the Aussies blow for blow. He was not prepared to take a step back. The Aussies were shaken by this approach because no other cricketer, let alone an Indian had taken them on this way. India used all the might they had. They almost pulled out of the Australian tour, got umpires replaced and even forced the International Cricket Council (ICC) to fly in their chief match referee Ranjan Madugalle to douse the fire. All this for one man, Harbhajan Singh!

India had been hurt and more importantly their most trusted soldier Harbhajan had been at the forefront of this battle.

Harbhajan was at the forefront of one more battle, this time with a fellow Indian cricketer, Sreesanth. It was alleged that Harbhajan slapped Sreesanth during the first edition of the Indian Premier League (IPL). Harbhajan was banned and missed the first full season of IPL.

For the Aussies, this behaviour was proof of what they felt had happened with Andrew Symonds Down Under. But Harbhajan wasn't one to be cowed down. He was getting ready for more such battles. He grew under Dhoni's leadership, spinning a few famous wins as well.

The crowning glory was obviously the 2011 World Cup, which was also the turning point in Harbhajan's career.

For most cricketers who played in that tournament, the win in Mumbai seemed like the pinnacle of their career. And everything else that followed appeared to be less dramatic. India went on a downhill curve from there on and it was not a surprise that Harbhajan started missing out.

I think the injury to Harbhajan on the 2011 England tour was symptomatic of the problems that befell Indian cricket. Harbhajan and a few others were just the face of the problems. India appeared to have taken the foot off the accelerator after winning the 2011 World Cup and was prepared to rest on their laurels. Ruthless sides like Australia would not have done that. Harbhajan may not have been the force he was but he still remained my hero.

Harbhajan's career suffered a big jolt after that injury he suffered in England. That in my view was a turning point in his career. He did make a couple of comebacks at the ICC World Twenty20 in 2012, then against England and Australia in 2012–13 much later in 2016 again for the World Twenty20, but he was sadly a forgotten man.

He even gave up captaincy at Mumbai Indians and his performance improved in the IPL. He reunited with his old foe Ponting at Mumbai Indians. But the sport was slowly seeing a feisty character fade away.

I have forever remained his admirer because he was the original spin doctor of Indian cricket. He never flinched and was forever prepared for a scrap. He was ready to get his hands dirty much like any creative person. He was skill and craft personified; India was privileged to have a sporting son like him.

***

Virender Sehwag

When India's cricket history is written, the names of the greatest openers usually find a place. The debate till Virender Sehwag came on the scene was limited to Vijay Merchant and Sunil Gavaskar.

But from the time he arrived, he made a compelling case for his name to be included among the top three.

In fact, Virender Sehwag surpassed all expectations and became one of the greatest players the country has produced. But things were not always that rosy. Sehwag came into the public view first in 1998 as a chubby teenager. He was then playing for the Indian under-19 side in the World Cup in South Africa.

There were few more youngsters in that side who went on to play for India. Sehwag with his off-breaks and sturdy approach with the bat caught the attention of a lot of people, especially the national selectors. The 1998–99 was a season of hope for Indian cricket, there were quite a few changes being observed. Some older players like Navjot Sidhu were all set to be junked forever.

Then the younger players were coming into their own. Rahul Dravid was finally being accepted as an all-weather cricketer. Some others like VVS Laxman were trying to find their feet. So the situation was fluid in the Indian cricket squad. After enjoying a fruitful 1998, again mostly at home, Mohammad Azharuddin's captaincy was once again under pressure.

In the midst of all this, began the usual tamasha in India around the World Cup, scheduled for May–June 1999. There was a lot of interest in the provisional squad that India would choose. One name that cropped up was that of Sehwag who was picked as an off-spinner and all-rounder. He was making waves with the Delhi Ranji Trophy side that season.

He was therefore picked purely on the basis of the selectors' gut feeling. The World Cup was preceded by a tri-series at home involving a rampant Pakistan and a struggling Sri Lanka. India got over the Lankan challenge easily, but it was the Pakistanis who were proving difficult to deal with. We had a number of injury issues and in the midst of all this, Sehwag was thrown into the deep end in Mohali.

Before he made his ODI debut, I remember waking up early one day to watch a breakfast show on Doordarshan.

He was an unknown character about whom not much was known. I thought to myself that he appeared very quietly confident, but doubted if he really had it in him to become a valuable member of the Indian cricket team. Sehwag was straightforward in his approach in that interview which impressed me.

The proof of how good he really was would only be known when he played for India. That call came soon because the spate of injuries meant that Sehwag was drafted in against Pakistan at Mohali for an ODI debut. The match is still bit of a blur because the series was a complete washout as far as the Indian side was concerned. The match was a foregone conclusion because the Pakistanis were just too good for a young Indian side.

Sehwag came in to bat in the middle-order, but struggled in the face of the extreme pace of Shoaib Akhtar. He had not seen anything remotely close to that either in age-group cricket or in domestic cricket. So to expect him to simply adjust to playing express pace was always going to be difficult. He was beaten by pace. Sehwag walked off the pitch and was completely forgotten for a couple of years.

Those two years were chaotic for Indian cricket with a number of forced and unforced changes in the team and in the leadership. India had gone through a turmoil that few sides had been through thanks mainly to external factors. It was hardly a surprise that the selectors decided to cast the net far and wide to get fresh talent.

Sehwag had not been completely forgotten, so he came back into the frame in 2001 when Australia stayed on to play an ODI series after a historic Test series. Sehwag made an instant impact this time with a brisk half-century and a useful spell with his off-breaks. He looked a loveable character with his chubby cheeks and made an instant impact netting a man of the match award. Unfortunately he injured his finger and was again out of public view for some time.

We did not hear much about Sehwag thereafter. The big change happened on the 2001 tour to Sri Lanka where a depleted Indian squad took the field. Sehwag was back in the mix after injury, he had to be fielded, so he opened the batting after the experiments with Amay Khurasiya failed miserably. Sehwag was called back to make up for the gaps in the line-up. This time too Sehwag was given a different role, but finally the think-tank decided to push him up the order to open the batting.

Yuvraj Singh had been tried as an opener in the ODI format before Sehwag was pushed into the role against New Zealand in a tri-series match on that Sri Lanka tour. India's batting had been struggling then, it needed a special effort from the willow to secure a place in the final.

And it happened, all thanks to the masterstroke to have Sehwag open the batting. He was simply devastating. I had not seen hitting of the kind since Sachin Tendulkar smashed the Kiwis when he first opened the batting in 1994 at Auckland. It was simply breath-taking as he scored a hundred at breakneck speed. Suddenly a lot of people realised that he batted just like his hero, Tendulkar. The styles were similar and anyone could have been mistaken him for the master batsman.

Next day, all the newspapers were gushing about this boy wonder from Najafgarh. The media descended on the little town just outside Delhi. The intricate details about how Viru began his career and how he journeyed to the Ferozeshah Kotla ground in Delhi became common knowledge. By now everyone knew that he liked to drink milk!

Even Tendulkar raised a toast to his protégé and things seemed to be going well for the young all-rounder. Sehwag was finally fast tracked into the Test XI, simply because of the potential he showed in the ODI matches. He made his Test debut in South Africa at Bloemfontein. When Sehwag joined Tendulkar at the crease, it took me some time to understand who was who! It was that difficult to differentiate between the master and his pupil. Even the commentators struggled to find a differentiating factor. Sehwag matched Tendulkar stroke for stroke and it was a sight to behold as he took on the best in the world.

He finally reached a well-deserved Test hundred on debut, the sign of things to come. For a man considered to be purely a limited-overs specialist, Sehwag surpassed all expectations. He not only managed to bring fresh hope to Indian cricket, but nearly also played a part in dividing world cricket forever. Sehwag was handed a one-match suspension for excess appealing, some others were fined and Tendulkar was hauled up for tampering with the ball. All this happened in the second Test.

India looked to cancel the rest of the tour if the referee Mike Denness was not replaced. The International Cricket Council (ICC) was caught between the devil and the deep blue sea. Long conversations, conference calls and attempts to mediate resulted in the third Test going ahead.

The only catch was the Test was going to be held with a Cricket South Africa (CSA) match referee and not Denness. ICC stripped the Test of its official status and the two sides played out a farcical first-class match! Sehwag, unknown to him, had brought world cricket to the edge.

Finally, before the next series at home, England, India and other key stakeholders managed to get the matter resolved. But the only compromise solution was that Sehwag would be banned for a Test. So in his very second series, against England, Sehwag started off with a ban!

Sehwag learnt his lessons well and from thereon made an impact in ODI cricket consistently. He was Tendulkar 2.0 in many ways and that created a big impact in the way India played in the 50-over format. The arrival of Sehwag created a problem of plenty at the top of the order in ODI cricket for India. Sourav Ganguly and Tendulkar had been India's ODI openers since 1996 but now there was a new claimant to the position. It created a fair bit of tension.

Sehwag was the one to take up the position. He brought a fresh approach which represented a young India wanting to take on the best in the world. He was not bogged down by reputations or his rivals. His approach was simple: see the ball, hit the ball.

He grew in stature on the English tour of 2002. Critics kept saying that Sehwag would be tested in England. But Sehwag did what he managed to do for more than a decade thereafter: prove all his critics wrong. In conditions that were meant to test, Sehwag was thrown a challenge which the young man took up. He was now being seen as a Test match opener too.

He smashed a hundred in his first Test as opener in 2002 in England, thereby underlining his value to the side. He was prepared to bite the bullet for the cause of the side. In the ODI format he continued to smash bowlers at will especially during the now famous tri-series in England in 2002. He was relentless in his approach. But behind the destructive batsman was a calm man who showed us the value of dealing with pressure in a unique way. He would sing songs to help reduce pressure. Can you imagine a bowler bowling at 90 miles per hour being confronted by a batsman who was singing a Hindi film song?

But that was Sehwag's personality.

He would carry his personality into any contest and that is what endeared him to the cricket-loving public of India. The next best moment in my view was during the 2003 World Cup against Pakistan. Three of the greatest fast bowlers of Pakistan — Waqar Younis, Wasim Akram and Shoaib Akhtar — were steaming in to bowl, but this man was nonchalant. Imagine Sehwag walking out with a song on his lips, while the whole of India was praying!

He smashed Akhtar over the point region to convey a telling statement in that match. That was a knockout blow for Pakistan from which they failed to recover. That was the beauty of the Sehwag magic. He would deliver these missiles which would flatten the best bowlers in the world.

This was the same man who was considered to be not good enough to play anything beyond a bit of one-day cricket. Now this same Sehwag was India's trump card while taking on the world. His next big achievement came in the Boxing Day Test at Melbourne in 2003. My friends and I got together at my place to watch the Test match. What we saw on the tube was something out of the world. With contrasting approaches, Sehwag and his stodgy partner Aakash Chopra achieved maximum returns. Sehwag smashed the Aussie bowlers all over the Melbourne Cricket Ground (MCG) that day. It was a sight to behold. He held no fear and that was the biggest lesson for us all.

Sehwag's belligerent approach was matched with a temperament which was extremely solid. He was prepared to take a chance even at the fag end of the day. That approach meant India gained a lot, even though Sehwag was criticised for not scoring beyond his magical knock of 195. The Aussies were visibly shaken. Even the unflappable Steve Waugh, playing his final Test series was shaken by the Sehwag assault. This was an approach that the Aussies had perfected, scoring at four runs an over in Test matches. Now, Sehwag was not just matching it, but sometimes even bettering it with his aggression. This was the perfect example of learning from the rivals and making them pay!

Sehwag's efforts went to nought in that MCG Test, but a pattern was emerging of how his batting was the key to India's fortunes in the oldest format of the game. This reputation gained further currency when India played their first Test in Pakistan since 1989. Before the start of the Test series, the ODI series was a bit of a highlight with fans pouring in from both countries to see the action. But when it came to the Test match in a far flung place like Multan, there were hardly any spectators on view. For an entertainer, to motivate himself in that situation was a tough task. But Sehwag surpassed all expectations. For a change, he even challenged Akhtar verbally and then went about smashing the other bowlers. His assault on the magical off-spinner of the 1990s, Saqlain Mushtaq, effectively ended the legend's career. The best part about Sehwag? It was his ability to react the same way in all situations. He moved from 294 to 300 with a six, which most Indian batsmen would have avoided. With that one shot, he smashed the long-held theories about how the batsmen from India could tackle the world. Sehwag was the most unlikely candidate to become the first Indian man to score a Test triple hundred. But he did that in style.

He seemed to love the Test match format very much. All his exploits were in Test matches. He seemed to reserve special love for the Aussies in the way he smashed them in Chennai during a series in 2004. More often than not because of the speed at which he batted, the other Indian batsmen failed to match him.

That continued to be the narrative for the next couple of years. In ODI cricket he seemed to falter or maybe he found the format to be less challenging because of the field setting. This was interesting because Sehwag was made for one-day cricket. Despite all these achievements, Sehwag's form started dropping.

Sometimes the lack of form in ODIs percolated into Tests and that made an attacking player like Sehwag ineffective. He lost his place quite often because when form deserted an influential player like Sehwag it became quite obvious.

However, even if he lost his place, each time he came back, Sehwag performed in sterling fashion. Whether it was in 2007–08 in Australia when he slammed a match-saving hundred or when he battered South Africa in Chennai to register India's highest individual Test score of 319, Sehwag knew how to answer his detractors.

He was not done yet because he smashed another double, this time against Sri Lanka in Mumbai at the Cricket Club of India. He narrowly missed out on a chance to hit three Test triple hundreds. He then followed it up with some belated exploits in ODI cricket.

He hit a double hundred in ODIs and then his counter-attack in the 2011 World Cup was the reason why India progressed as far as they did. His approach especially in the semi-finals, won me over completely. Yet again, like in 2003, Sehwag was nonchalant as he took on Pakistan's best bowler Umar Gul in the semi-final in Mohali. I was in the crowd watching with nervous energy, but this guy just did not get flustered. He took Gul on and set the stage for India. That tactic worked wonders. He was an ideal lieutenant to all the captains.

He was street smart, but also honest in his approach so he was known to speak his mind. Whether it was while taking on the bowlers and fielders or while commenting on his host Bangladesh's lack of ability to win Test matches, Sehwag was brutal. That was the quality about Sehwag which showed that he did not carry any baggage of the past. He had clarity of thought which enabled him to look at scores, whether it was 99, 199 or 299 as just mere numbers. There is a tendency amongst a lot of people to stress out and get overawed. But if there was anything that Sehwag taught all of us then it was to be unfazed by the situation on hand. It paid him rich dividends.

It is no surprise that India's most productive years from 2002 to 2009 coincided with the presence of Sehwag at the top of the order. Since then, India has been below par only because Sehwag started dropping form, especially in Test matches.

He was followed by the reliable Rahul Dravid and together they changed the face of Indian Test batting. For me both Sehwag and Dravid are two of India's best ever Test batsmen.

I think not enough credit is given to Sehwag the off-spinner because with his drift he was able to trouble a lot of batsmen, especially the likes of Adam Gilchrist. His spell in the 2008 Perth Test is still rated highly by a lot of critics. It was a pity that we did not see more of Sehwag as a bowler or captain. It was India's loss.

The way Sehwag went out of international cricket was a bit disappointing. He lost form rapidly after the end of the 2011 World Cup, but this time he was not able to strike it rich again. He was a shadow of his former self and that was a telling sign. It was not the same Sehwag who had won hearts world over. It was hardly a surprise then that Sehwag went out without much of a fanfare. He never got an opportunity to bid goodbye to the world of cricket. Instead he was cast away into the obscurity of domestic cricket. That was a sad commentary on the way we handled our stars.

For a batsman who redefined the art of batting and set new standards for himself, the exit from the sport was a bit tame.

Maybe there is a lesson in it for all of us.

***

Zaheer Khan

It was by chance that I happened to read the city round-up of cricketing action in *The Times of India* in 1996. There was a local club tournament going on in Mumbai which drew my attention to the effusive praise that was reserved for one man.

A few days later that same man was called up to bowl at the Indian squad just before the final of the Titan Cup. He had impressed one man, Sanjay Manjrekar, who had a fancy for fast bowlers, being an unabashed admirer of Pakistani cricket. Manjrekar had scored lots of runs against the Pakistan pace attack in his early years but respected their ability with the ball. In Zaheer Khan, he saw something similar.

However, it took some more time before Zaheer actually made his first-class debut. He was from the interior of Maharashtra and was studying to be an engineer. He made his debut for Baroda, though because the Mumbai Ranji Trophy team had a lot of bowling options. Zaheer had no other go but to move states to try his luck.

It was in the 1999–2000 season that we first saw him being spoken about as a future Indian fast bowler. He was quickly drafted into an India 'B' side that toured Oman for a tournament. This side was captained by an out-of-favour Nayan Mongia, also Zaheer's Baroda teammate. Then there was another left-arm bowler in the side, Sachin Nair of Maharashtra. Together, they were expected to be the new talents that India was seeking in the fast bowling department. Those were the days when the world was singing praises of Shoaib Akhtar and Brett Lee as they rattled batsmen with their pace.

India was crying out for a pace bowler of their own. But we were constantly being reminded by one and all that we are not a nation made for fast bowlers. Twenty-five years after Kapil Dev faced similar taunts, nothing had changed. India was going through a crisis in their cricket with the taint of match-fixing marring their superstars. In the midst of all this Zaheer was called up for a pre-Asia Cup camp in Pune in June 2000. But when the squad was finally chosen, Zaheer was not picked. There were reports then that the captain Sourav Ganguly wanted Zaheer in the mix, but it was not to be.

The match-fixing scandal toppled a couple of our superstars. Indian cricket was in a state of flux and looking to break away from the shady past. Ganguly got his wish, and the young left-arm pacer was finally picked for the ICC Champions Trophy in Kenya. Zaheer's selection raised the hopes of a lot of people. Much had been spoken about his speed and his ability to bowl yorkers. India started off well in the practice matches and you could tell that Zaheer was the cynosure of all eyes. It was strange to see so much interest being shown in an Indian fast bowler, but it was also a moment of pride for us.

When the tournament proper started, Zaheer yorked his way into the minds of a number of Indian fans as he destroyed the hosts. Then in the next two encounters he got the better of some of the best cricketers from South Africa and Australia. His delivery to Steve Waugh marked a massive attitudinal shift in the way India's fast bowlers were looked at by the world.

Thereafter, however Zaheer appeared to lose a bit of sting. He seemed to conserve his energy as he bowled. The zest shown by him in his debut tournament appeared to be missing, as he drifted along for a bit. Except seeing him smash Zimbabwe's Henry Olonga for successive sixes there was nothing much of note from Zaheer for almost a year and a half. Like many others before him, Zaheer appeared to be a false dawn in Indian cricket. Numerous examples went through my mind as I saw Zaheer trundling in rather than steaming in after the 2000 Champions Trophy.

I was particularly concerned because Zaheer was India's biggest fast bowling hope.

But it all changed in 2002 when India's brilliant run in overseas Test matches began. Zaheer started to play a big role in the wins, striking early. He was unlike the other Indian fast bowlers in the past, in that he seemed to make things happen. That was a rare quality for an Indian fast bowler to have. He seemed to enjoy bowling and always appeared to be in rhythm.

I was particularly overjoyed when we won the Test in Headingley, Leeds. Zaheer led from the front very well. You could see very soon that he liked being the leader of the pack. He continued to impress till we entered the World Cup in 2003. Here too he was the third cog of a three-pronged pace attack that also included Javagal Srinath and Ashish Nehra. I think India probably had their best pace attack ever assembled for the 2003 World Cup.

A young zippy Zaheer, a slinging Nehra, a wily Srinath and a bouncy Ajit Agarkar sitting on the bench. Then there were the two champion spin bowlers Anil Kumble and Harbhajan Singh. There was a competition between the two spinners too for a place in the playing XI. Indian cricket never had it so good in terms of bowling potential.

Zaheer struck vital blows and India did well in the tournament. But it was in the final, that he showed his inexperience. The way he sledged the Australian openers Matthew Hayden and Adam Gilchrist did not bode well for the team. Zaheer lost the plot, and the rest as they say, is history. Zaheer was clearly wiser for the experience. He never repeated those mistakes again.

Whenever he took on the batsmen thereafter he was the one challenging them with the ball. He made the most of his skills and tried to always build on it. He was never one to be satisfied with what he had naturally. I was particularly impressed by the way he took on the responsibility of being the number one fast bowler after the retirement of Srinath. He was keen to make a contribution and was prepared to go the extra yard.

In Australia in 2003–04 for example, he rattled the Aussies in a short sharp spell in Brisbane to underline his value to the side. But injuries constantly dogged him and stalled his progress through his crucial years. I hated the spectacle during the 2004 Asia Cup when he was less than fit, but was being put through the grind by the team medical staff at the last minute.

It did not augur well for a number one fast bowler to be chosen to play despite being less than fit. I felt those were crucial years where Zaheer did not get to maximise his potential. Thereafter, in 2005 he got into a scrap with the then coach Greg Chappell. It was clearly a clash of ideas. Zaheer was the number one fast bowler who wanted to do it his way, Chappell felt he needed to get more from his numero uno strike bowler. The fact was that in the 2005–06 season, Zaheer clearly looked like he had put on a lot of weight. The zip was missing. In Test matches he seemed to struggle to bowl the second and third spells. All that put together painted a grim picture of what was in store for Indian cricket when the premier fast bowler was not up to the mark.

Zaheer very soon lost his place in the Indian Test and ODI sides. Younger fast bowlers took his place and made an immediate impact.

This was when Zaheer turned the corner in his career. He signed a county contract with Worcestershire and bowled over after over in the 2006 English summer. He picked up truckloads of wickets for the English county side, so much so that he even came close to taking all 10 wickets in an innings. Zaheer was making headlines in England for all the right reasons. It was hardly a surprise that at the end of the season he would be an automatic choice for the Indian squad.

He was fitter now, slimmer and appeared to have become smarter with the ball. He now seem relaxed in his skin and was making the ball talk at will. Even the legendary Wasim Akram felt like he was watching a prototype of himself in action. That was great praise.

Zaheer's willingness to improve, change and learn impressed me no end. Here was a cricketer who was written off by all, yet he came back in style to rebuild his career. He made an instant impact. He rattled the Englishmen in 2007 when India claimed their first series win in Old Blighty since 1986! Zaheer was the big difference between the two sides. It helped that the English fielders needled him by placing jelly beans near the stumps when he came out to bat. Zaheer noticed it and realised it was a slight, because they could not believe that he could move the ball so much without using unfair means. Zaheer felt that his integrity was being questioned. It brought the best out of him and he ran through the English line-up.

For Zaheer being provoked was one way of motivating himself to do better.

It worked yet again when Australia came calling in 2008–09. Their wicket-keeper Brad Haddin got into a verbal duel with Zaheer which fired him up and took what was a legendary pötshot at the Aussies for slowing down in their batting. Zaheer rattled them with the ball thereafter. He was now the leader of the pack who was well and truly established in his role. Zaheer particularly loved mentoring Ishant Sharma. It was almost like an elder brother talking to his younger sibling. There was respect both ways and Ishant seemed to flower under Zaheer's tutelage. India gained from this *jugalbandi* as Zaheer loved his mentoring role.

You could see that he was a natural at sharing knowledge with his colleagues. He would stand at mid-off or mid-on and talk to the young bowlers who were coming through the system. It was almost Imran Khanesque in operation, and Zaheer loved this role. He had spent close to a decade in international cricket, and it made sense for him to share what he had learnt the hard way. With the ball too he was a master. He became an inspiration for not just Indian bowlers, but even overseas bowler James Anderson praised the effect Zaheer had on his bowling. That is high praise indeed because Anderson has turned out to be England's greatest-ever bowler. Zaheer's rise in stature from 2007–2011 was significant.

This showed that he was prepared to understand the demands of his body. He was no longer a teenager, so he had to respect the limitations that come with growing old. His mastering of his skills at a late stage of his career showed the value of keeping one's mind open. His performances coincided with Mahendra Singh Dhoni growing in stature as captain.

This is significant because Zaheer contributed majorly by marshalling the bowlers.

It was Zaheer's tremendous skills that resulted in him finishing as the leading wicket-taker in the 2011 World Cup. His spells, especially in the game against England, turned the tide in India's favour. I could never have imagined any other bowler having the kind of impact that Zaheer had in the tournament. He single-handedly carried India into the final with his bowling abilities. He struck early blows, controlled the flow of runs in the middle overs and then finally stifled the batsmen in the end overs.

It ensured that India was able to manage their opponents well throughout the tournament. He became a rallying point for India and that was the biggest highlight of Zaheer's career. He had moved a notch above his predecessor Srinath, who was also a lone warrior with the ball at times. Zaheer had the will to convert the opportunity into success. If Zaheer had similar results like Srinath then his career too would have been one of an underachiever. Zaheer managed to pull through the tough times and made the most of not having a consistent partner at all times.

After the 2011 World Cup high, Zaheer was not the same anymore. It was a painful sight to see Zaheer walk off on the first day of the Lord's Test in 2011 with an injury. Indian cricket suffered a massive setback and the results dropped. That was the impact of one man on India's cricketing fortunes. It demonstrated that despite having some of the world's best batsmen for teams it was still about taking wickets!

Zaheer did return but he was not the wily campaigner from before the 2011 World Cup. He had become a shadow of his former self, but there were sparks of his old days from time to time. One thing that Zaheer did was that he helped Dhoni mature into a leader. Zaheer would know where to bowl, how to bowl and knew his field settings well. Dhoni struggled after Zaheer left the scene, because the younger bowlers did not have the same understanding as the great man. He was left to set the field for the younger bowlers. But in the time that Zaheer was in the ranks, the bowling department was taken care of. He was almost the de facto bowling coach that the younger bowlers would look up to and try to learn from.

When Zaheer did come back for one final time, he had become fitter, but the zip in his bowling was missing. He could not beat the batsmen the way he would have in his heyday. Clearly the years of bowling were taking its toll on Zaheer's body. He was not a spring chicken anymore and the newest set of bowlers had come through. He could sense that his time was coming to a close as his mind was willing, but body was not. India lost his services yet again in 2014 and this time for good.

He was without doubt the greatest Indian fast bowler ever. No other fast bowler managed to have the same impact on India's results. He won Test matches for India and proved to the world that India could produce match-winning quick bowlers. His biggest impact was in creating an impression on the minds of young Indian boys and even girls. He inspired a generation of left-arm fast bowlers who have now come up in various parts of India. It is similar to the impact that Imran Khan created in Pakistan by first himself performing, then bringing on board the likes of Wasim Akram and Waqar Younis. Together that Pakistan trio made a major impact on Pakistan's cricketing fortunes. Zaheer's impact is something similar.

Now, when you see Zaheer bowl and lead Delhi Daredevils in the Indian Premier League (IPL) you get a sense of his valuable contribution to Indian cricket.

India is today poorer because he has retired, but I think we need to utilise his skills as a fast bowling coach. Imagine a day when Rahul Dravid is head coach and Zaheer Khan is the fast bowling coach. Indian cricket cannot ask for a better dream team than this to take the game forward.

***

Yuvraj Singh

In January 2000, when India's under-19 World Cup side travelled to Sri Lanka not many paid much attention to it. There was no hype around the squad like you have nowadays.

When India won the tournament, for the first-time ever the reactions were over the top. Some of the players like Mohammad Kaif and Reetinder Singh Sodhi had been in the news before as winners of the under-15 World Cup. But this time it was quite different.

There was however one man, rather boy, who caught the attention of quite a few people. It was a strong Punjab boy who was at the centre of it all. His name was Yuvraj Singh, son of former Indian fast bowler Yograj.

Now, Yograj was this well-built fast bowler who was Kapil Dev's batch mate. He played for India on the 1980–81 Australia and New Zealand tour. Thereafter, he went off the radar and would pop up on the scene to make some anti-Kapil comments. Then Yograj went into Punjabi movies and became a much loved actor.

Unknown to many, Yograj was training his son to be a cricketer. Stories about how he got Yuvraj moved out of skating, where he was doing well, to cricket started doing the rounds even as the under-19 World Cup of 2000 ended. He was then one of the most sought after Young Turks. A lot of those young boys were immediately drafted into one of the sides for the Challenger Trophy, a national one-day selection tournament. It was a big step up for most of the boys.

Yuvraj was being earmarked for bigger glory, but he was not immediately drafted into the ODI squad. He had to wait for another six months before that call came from the national selectors. He had shown that he has the promise, now it was about converting it. He was quietly waiting in the wings even as Indian cricket was going through a churning process. The likes of Mohammad Azharuddin and Ajay Jadeja had been banned following their alleged involvement in match-fixing. Then there were others who went out of favour. Very soon, Indian cricket had a situation where they had a young captain with a younger side to command.

This was a situation tailor-made for Yuvraj and the others like Zaheer Khan to showcase their talent. In the case of Yuvraj he got the opportunity on the biggest stage possible, the ICC Champions Trophy in 2000. He blasted his way into the hearts and minds of billions of Indians worldwide. The way he batted in the tournament, especially his knock of 84 against Australia, set him up for bigger things.

From there on it was the start of a journey that continued to reach newer heights. After the debut season there was a bit of a lull in Yuvraj's career. He sort of went off the radar. The senior pros like VVS Laxman and Rahul Dravid began asserting themselves. It was not until the 2001–02 ODI against Zimbabwe at Hyderabad that Yuvraj really asserted himself. That was the first time the Yuvraj-Mohammad Kaif partnership was played out on the international stage. Yuvraj's effort there set up a chance for India to win the ODI series against Zimbabwe, then a combative side of some note.

Yuvraj grew from that knock and became almost an indispensable member of the ODI set-up. So much so that to ensure that he got to play, the Indian think-tank asked Dravid to keep wickets. This enabled India to have a long batting line-up with Yuvraj at number six or seven shoring up the late order.

It worked wonders for India because they won the ODI series in West Indies for the first-time ever. Then in England during the now famous tri-series, Yuvraj shone with the bat. He did well both times at Lord's. He first came to the fore in the opening game of the tournament in the company of Dravid. Then in the final he extricated India out of trouble. India needed to chase about 326 with more than half the side back in the pavilion.

Yuvraj's efforts with Kaif is now part of cricketing folklore. I did not move an inch from the sofa while the chase was on. When India finally got over the finishing line, I remember jumping up in joy much like Sourav Ganguly in the Lord's balcony. That is a moment etched in my memory forever. I will never forget the celebrations that followed.

I had not celebrated like that till the win over Pakistan in the 2003 World Cup. That day at Centurion, the effortless ease with which Yuvraj smashed the Pakistan bowlers was just simply superb. The way he took on the ageing warhorses like Wasim Akram and Waqar Younis was a sight to behold. There was a lot of talk around the 2003 World Cup about the new India. Well, the biggest example of that was Yuvraj Singh and the ease with which he smashed the Pakistan bowling.

Yuvraj's biggest test was obviously going to be the Test match format. There was a growing feeling in the Indian cricket circles that maybe Yuvraj was not ready for the rigours of Test cricket. Extreme pace and the moving ball were claimed to be his bugbears. He struggled for a bit in New Zealand, when even the rest of the squad caved in. He eventually made his Test debut in October 2003, but he was always considered to be a limited-overs specialist.

India fought their way through in the 2003–04 season especially in Australia where Yuvraj stunned the fans Down Under with his majestic approach in the ODI format. Later, when India toured Pakistan, Yuvraj once again showed his prowess, but this time surprisingly in a Test match at Lahore's Gaddafi Stadium. He was sublime in a losing effort, but he showed that he had the talent to play the longest format of the game. The bigger problem in the Test match format was the fact that there was no vacancy in the middle order. Yuvraj struggled because the galacticos of Indian cricket took their appointed positions and did so for a major part of his career.

Yuvraj could either open or bat in the middle order. So Yuvraj took the bait and opened the batting. It lasted for all of three Test matches and that too against Australia. That was the only way Yuvraj could have fitted into the Test XI, so he took that option. He struggled for a bit and showed glimpses of what he was capable of in the second Test at Chennai in 2004–05. However, Indian cricket was quick to junk the experiment. Yuvraj has never opened again in any format and thankfully so. It was a sight however to watch two belligerent guys, Yuvraj and Virender Sehwag, opening the batting in a Test match for India.

Yuvraj continued to be under the radar as newer heroes came through. The rise of Mahendra Singh Dhoni meant that the role of the entertainer and finisher was handed over to the dashing Jharkhand man. Together however Dhoni and Yuvraj managed to stitch a number of stands in the limited-overs games which helped India get over difficult chases. The season of 2005–06 particularly was good for India while chasing precisely because of the presence of Dhoni and Yuvraj. Both were similar in styles with their power and their ability to clear the ropes. I particularly enjoyed their stands in Pakistan that season.

They came in tough chases and India managed to win an ODI series mainly because of this duo.

He continued to rise in stature, and by now was also one of the men marked by the coach Greg Chappell. The former Australian captain did not like the group of young boys brought in by Sourav Ganguly. So when Ganguly went out, his next target was the likes of Harbhajan, Yuvraj, Zaheer Khan and Ashish Nehra. But what Chappell managed with Zaheer and Nehra, he could not with Yuvraj. He tried very hard, but Yuvraj and also Harbhajan were performers. In the case of Yuvraj, he was a match-winner in the ODI format, so it was difficult to ignore his presence.

Yuvraj had now become a regular fixture in the ODI XI. However, before a crucial game against Australia in the 2006 Champions Trophy, he injured his knee thanks to a game of kho-kho, which was part of a training routine. I can still recall those images of Yuvraj writhing in pain and feeling bad for the man. He was India's go-to man, but he struggled and so did Dravid & Co. Without Yuvraj in the middle, the ODI XI looked half the side. It thereafter became a matter of speculation if Yuvraj could make it to the World Cup in the Caribbean.

I can recall going to the BKC ground of the Mumbai Cricket Association (MCA) and looking at Yuvraj limbering up and down. He was being constantly watched by the selectors and the team management. He was being put to the test and thankfully just before the selection of the squad, Yuvraj came through. He was declared fit and there was a collective sigh of relief, because he was that important to the billions of Indians.

The World Cup ended in a disaster, but the events of the few weeks before it, first the Chappell incident and the injury to

Yuvraj, meant that the left-hander dropped down the pecking order. He did not have much to do on the twin tours of Ireland and England. He was not involved in the Test XIs, so it was more in the ODI XIs that he showed his value.

Then came a turning point in Yuvraj's career which has now come to define him. He was named vice-captain of the first side to take part in the inaugural World Twenty20 in 2007 in South Africa. With the emergence of Dhoni, Yuvraj was now relegated to being the vice-captain and not the leader as many would have expected him to be. He was not however going to let himself be affected. As one of the senior players, Yuvraj was expected to be a leader in many ways. He really had it in for Stuart Broad who he smashed for six sixes. The background of the whole episode was that Yuvraj had been sledged by Andrew Flintoff in that crucial game at Durban against England. Yuvraj got needled and he answered in the best way possible.

It was a sight to watch him take on the English boys. That was the sort of tournament for Yuvraj, who really played a huge part in creating the Dhoni magic as captain. Yuvraj played a few more crucial knocks, but it was the Broad smash that he is remembered for even now. India won the tournament and it was the start of a new era. Dhoni-Yuvraj were given charge of the limited-overs squad. Together they brought in a fresh approach, bringing a close to the pre-2007 World Cup era. They were the men in charge in many ways and they together did a job similar to Ganguly-Dravid pairing. But even as this happened Yuvraj's form started deserting him. He scored a brilliant Test hundred against Pakistan in his return to the Test side in 2007–08. But the pressure grew as the rest of the world began talking about his dipping form. Everyone started talking about his personal life and he lost his hard-earned place in the Test XI. Yuvraj had been dealt with in a harsh manner by Test cricket. But he continued to fight to regain his place.

It was not until later in 2008 that he came back to the Test XI by right. He made an instant impact following the retirement of Ganguly. Yuvraj played a huge part in India's chase in Chennai against England. All the focus was always on the efforts by Tendulkar and Sehwag in that Chennai chase, but it was Yuvraj as well who played a part in that emotional match post the Mumbai attacks. Yuvraj was now back in the fray in all formats, because of the departure of a few legends.

The whole of India was building towards the 2011 World Cup which was to be staged at home. And so was Yuvraj. By now he was slowly becoming a key factor in India's plans. He was no longer the vice-captain, but one of the most important players in Dhoni's plans. It was also his left-arm spin that was going to play a big part in the tournament for India. In the interim phase, Yuvraj lost his place yet again in the Test XI. This was quite disappointing because Yuvraj's Test career had been a stop-start because of the presence of the legends. But he failed to build on the opportunities that came his way. Maybe he was not hungry enough to stamp his authority on the format like he did in the ODIs.

But it was the 2011 World Cup that was going to define Yuvraj's career. He did not disappoint anyone in the tournament. He was India's trump card with the bat and ball. His knock especially against West Indies at Chennai was worth its weight in gold. With the ball, he picked crucial wickets and provided the all-rounder's touch that the Indian limited-overs side has lacked since. He was the go-to man for MS Dhoni in the tournament. He was simply unstoppable. It seemed that four years on Yuvraj had not aged a day as he went about stamping his authority on the tournament. Along with Zaheer Khan, Yuvraj was the top bowler in terms of wickets taken for India. That was quite an achievement. It was Yuvraj who made an impact in almost all the games, except the final.

In the final it was the captain Dhoni who took the challenge upon himself to steer the chase, but Yuvraj was around when Dhoni hit the winning six. That moment and the sight of a teary-eyed Yuvraj hugging Dhoni and Tendulkar will be remembered by billions of Indians forever.

I was watching the final with a few friends and remember every moment of the match. Suffice to say I was a proud Indian that night. I learnt a few things about Yuvraj during the tournament. He was dependable and was always willing to deliver under pressure.

For very long Yuvraj had the image of being a flamboyant social butterfly, but all that changed with the kind of mature show that he put up during the World Cup.

What we as a nation and fans did not know was that, Yuvraj had been suffering during the World Cup. Even as he was scripting history, Yuvraj was vomiting blood! It was the start of his long tryst with the dreaded cancer. Yuvraj endured the pain and played for few more months, before 'injury' put him out of the England tour of 2011 completely. It was not until later that the reality of the situation and the grave nature of his illness came to the fore. He rose in my estimation in this phase simply because of the fact that he bravely endured the illness for the nation.

Very few individuals managed to gain as much goodwill as Yuvraj in this phase. Yuvraj was sadly never the same cricketer. He went through treatment in the United States of America and he even had a book written and a TV documentary made on his struggles. He came back in style and when he did, there was concern about how he would cope with the rigours of international cricket.

Everyone felt like one of their own had been afflicted by a killer disease. Thankfully, Yuvraj had managed to push back the menace and made an emotional return to the sport he loved. It seemed like the selectors and team management too were keen to provide him a second chance. He was back in every possible format, including the Test matches.

But it was not for long. India lost its patience with Yuvraj again, this time finally when it lost to England in the Test series at home in 2012–13. That was the end of Yuvraj as a Test cricketer. He had never come close to being a Test match cricketer. India then lost an important ODI series to Pakistan at home also in the same season. It was only in the T20I format that India managed to have faith in Yuvraj.

Yuvraj had been dropping in estimation by the day in all formats for India. Very soon, Yuvraj was out of the ODI squad for good and has not played for India since then. It was a pity because Yuvraj was meant to be India's superstar in the 50-over format. But a variety of factors like injury, illness and form meant that he kept dropping out of favour.

It was sad that Yuvraj's all-round skills did not come in use especially at the 2015 World Cup. He was always going to be a better bet than any of the other left-hand spinner all-rounders that India has in their mix right now. Somehow, the selectors and more importantly the think-tank do not seem to have the belief.

I was particularly pained to see the struggle of Yuvraj in the T20I format. He really took time to stamp his authority at the World Twenty20 in 2014 in Bangladesh. In seven years how much had changed, the man who ruled the format in the inaugural tournament in 2007 was finding it difficult to get the ball off the square in the tournament. The match against West Indies was a sight that I do not want to remember ever. The low, slow pitches of Bangladesh got the better of him. It affected him so much that in the final, one of the prime reasons for India losing was that they lost momentum when Yuvraj batted.

It was a sorry sight and no one's fault. It so happens that when belligerent batsmen lose form, they go off the radar rather quickly. You saw that happening to Virender Sehwag as well. I was disappointed in the way Yuvraj ended the tournament, but satisfied that I had seen some of his best exploits in flesh and sometimes on television.

India missed Yuvraj majorly in the ODI format, but the fact is that it was a younger version of the left-handed champion that we missed. He was no longer the crown prince, he was expected to have become the king, but he somehow failed to grab the opportunity that came his way. He did not end up having the career a lot of us expected him to have.

He needed to have done a lot more. Unfortunately, in the case of Yuvraj, his off-field life seemed to garner more eyeballs. But he was that kind of personality. India perhaps did not know how to handle him. In the time we did do that, we got the best out of him in at least the limited-overs format. He did come back into the squad for the World Twenty20 in 2016, but it was clear that he was not at his best.

Yuvraj for me lived up to his name of being a prince, but it is sad that he did not graduate to become a Maharaj!

***

Mahendra Singh Dhoni

It was around the year 2002 that I first read the name of a young Jharkhand boy. The reports gushed about the boy. But again I did not give it too much credence, though the name Mahendra Singh Dhoni got stuck in my head.

He continued to make waves in domestic cricket and one could see that the selectors kept an eye on him in the way they gave him chances. He was now being discussed at selection committee meetings. The fact that he was being discussed meant that the selectors were serious about the young man. It did not take long for the selectors to select him for the Indian team.

There were lots of reports of the selectors being stonewalled by the-then captain Sourav Ganguly. The fact that there was another wicket-keeper in the national reckoning like Deep Dasgupta, who incidentally hailed from Bengal like Ganguly, meant that Dhoni's India call was delayed.

The closest he came to being called up by India was before the 2003–04 tour to Pakistan. The selectors actively considered picking him. I was by now intrigued by the man. Just who was this man that the cricketing community in India was so actively pushing?

This was the first time that someone who was not in the national squad was being rated so highly. I remember then keeping a track of Dhoni. I thought to myself if this man has the ability that people keep talking about then he will change the face of Indian cricket forever. It almost seemed like stars were aligning themselves well to help Dhoni catapult into superstardom.

It was the 2004 tour to Kenya and Zimbabwe by India 'A'. The squad had two wicket-keepers but it was Dhoni who was being keenly followed. I remember the one-dayers in Kenya especially where Dhoni just let himself go. I have never seen hitting of that kind ever in my years of watching international cricket. Dhoni simply stole my heart that day as I watched the game on the television.

India was struggling to find a regular wicket-keeper batsman since the departure of Nayan Mongia.

The selectors' hands were forced by the losses to Australia. So in came Dinesh Karthik in the Test matches. India's next ODI was not until December 2004 when they were to tour Bangladesh.

It was expected that the selectors would finally blood Dhoni for the ODI segment of the tour. Dhoni walked in with a smile, with his long flowing hair and immediately caught everyone's attention.

The series against Bangladesh itself was not worth remembering, because apart from Dhoni there was nothing much to talk about.

Again, luckily India's ODI squad was going through a lull in the format. The selectors had earmarked Dinesh Karthik to take over the Test gloves and Dhoni for ODIs. It seemed a perfectly common sense decision. But this was not going to last for long.

I decided to fly to Vizag to watch India play Pakistan, because we do not get much of that contest in our beloved

Mumbai. In the end it turned out to be a very wise decision because that day Dhoni absolutely smashed the Pakistan bowlers. It was carnage of the highest order with brute force on display. For an Indian supporter, this was almost Richardsesque in style. It had a devastating effect. Pakistan could not recover that day from the Dhoni brutality. It was very clear from thereon that Dhoni would be the chosen one for India in the ODI format. He had well and truly taken over the role in pyjama cricket. Dhoni soon became a marketing man's delight, he kept growing his hair and his stories gained currency.

Whether it was about Dhoni drinking milk or whether it was his passion for bikes or dogs, India warmed up to the new superstar. Amidst all the upheaval in Indian cricket in 2005, Dhoni stood firm because it was not his place to get involved in disputes between the legends of cricket. He quietly gained prominence and was one of the most destructive players India possessed.

His biggest moment came when the Sri Lankans came calling. The unbeaten knock of 183 at Jaipur really catapulted him onto another level. This was the second blockbuster effort in 2005 from the Ranchi man. It made a big impact in the way India looked at Dhoni. He had managed to go to the next level and the selectors were keen to observe that climb up the ladder.

So when the selectors had to choose a wicket-keeper for the Tests, they were quick to dump Karthik for Dhoni. It was clear that Dhoni was at a different level from his competitors. None of his rivals for the gloves had made the sort of impact that Dhoni did. It was not long before the 2005–06 season was Dhoni's in the ODI format. He was the one who created the most impact with the bat and on the field (behind the stumps). He was the reason why India grew as an ODI squad. Then came the Pakistan tour where he really grew in stature and gained the respect of his peers. The way Dhoni tackled the likes of Shoaib Akhtar in the Faisalabad Test was a sight to behold.

A rampaging fast bowler Shoaib was running in at breakneck speed to do just that, break the neck. But Dhoni was equal to the task as he battled fire with fire. The way he hooked and pulled that day was simply unbelievable. I think that knock was Dhoni's reason to be counted among the stars of Indian cricket at the time. Then in the ODIs, he stole the show by playing a part in countering Pakistan's totals. His hair had turned golden and was long and flowing. He now had many admirers including a certain General Pervez Musharraf, former president of Pakistan. I still remember chuckling as I saw Musharraf telling Dhoni not to cut his hair! That was the topic of debate in those days as Dhoni walked around with that strut of his.

India was quickly embracing a hero of their own, who was the new age superstar. He was much bigger than the phenomenon of Sachin Tendulkar. This guy represented the new young Indian but from the interiors of the country. He was sharp and in the words of Greg Chappell, the former Indian coach, a future leader, when speaking during the England series at a function in Jamshedpur to felicitate Dhoni. How prophetic Chappell was as Dhoni slowly but surely climbed up the ladder.

It was not long before the World Cup 2007 ended in a disaster leading to a lot of heartburn in India, because we cry about nothing else except an early exit from the mega event! Indian fans wanted nothing short of some blood for the early exit. They were seething with anger. The selectors rung the changes, made a few tough calls by leaving out a few of the stars. Dhoni was catapulted into the role of being the vice-captain of the ODI side. The selectors were clearly seeing him as future captain, at least in the ODI format.

The next big moment for Dhoni came when he single-handedly saved India from a certain defeat in the first Test at Lord's in 2007 against England. India was surely hurtling towards defeat when Dhoni came to bat. But a combination of rain, poor umpiring and some comical Sreesanth batting, we were saved. India went on to win the series for the first time and no praise can be too high for Dhoni. His approach was tremendous. It was quite unlike Dhoni to play a stubborn, stodgy innings. But he changed his stripes and gained instant results.

Dhoni was slowly but surely inching towards the leader's crown. He was then named captain of the team to play the first-ever World Twenty20 in South Africa. It was a young team with a number of senior players being recalled. Dhoni was clearly seen as the leader of the generation next. It was a curious campaign. A squad assembled as an afterthought, which gathered at the Johannesburg airport stunned the world. More importantly it was the cool approach of Dhoni that caught everyone's attention.

Whether it was in that tense encounter against Pakistan in the league stage or the matches against England, South Africa or Australia, Dhoni never appeared flustered. He was calm and in fact seemed to revel in the role. It was during this tournament that India's regular captain Rahul Dravid resigned from his role to once again throw our cricket into turmoil. It was not long before the selectors anointed Dhoni as the new captain.

I was watching this development keenly because Dhoni led a young side to the World Twenty20 title, but to lead a side of champions like Tendulkar, Ganguly and Dravid would be a tough task. But somehow once the celebrations of winning the World Twenty20 ended, reality struck all of us. Dhoni was now the uncrowned king of Indian cricket, quite a feat considering that the champions were still very much around. India continued to grow in the ODI format that season. Dhoni showed his ruthless streak for the first time when he dropped his first two captains, Ganguly and Dravid, from the ODI squad for the tri-series in Australia.

India managed to win the tri-series in Australia for the first-time ever and it was quite a big upset because till then the host side had been an undisputed world champion in the format. But despite these successes, the selectors were not keen to push Dhoni as Test captain. They played with care and caution, instead by naming Anil Kumble, that battle-scarred veteran, as the leader at the fag end of his career. Dhoni, however, got a chance to lead India in Tests when Kumble was out injured and in his very first match in charge, he registered a win at Kanpur in 2008 against South Africa!

Dhoni's brand value further increased with the advent of the Indian Premier League (IPL). But I was more focussed on his performances for the Indian team, because that was what mattered in the end. For the first time in over three years Dhoni opted out of a Test series during the Sri Lanka tour in 2008. But it was not long before Dhoni would get the role to captain India in the Test match format later that very year.

Just two months down the road India would have its next full-time Test captain in Dhoni when Kumble retired following an injury. Dhoni managed to surpass all expectations and won both the Tests he led in the series against Australia! Again despite a loss of the senior players, Dhoni was slowly gaining prominence as Test captain.

He did not lose a single Test series for the first four years of being in charge of the side. His best year in Test cricket was in 2009 when he led India to their first series win in New Zealand since 1967. Then later in 2009, India became the number one Test side in the world. That was a proud moment for a number of Indians, especially the likes of Ganguly and Dravid who had played a big part in changing the mind-set of the Test squads over the years.

India was also managing to constantly battle and hold onto the number one position in Test cricket. The best moment came in South Africa in the run-up to the World Cup when India finished the series 1-1. That was a big achievement for an Indian squad not expected to hurt a fly. A lot of credit goes to Dhoni for the achievement.

Then in the World Cup that followed everyone knows how Dhoni changed the face of India's approach in the tournament with his calm demeanour. Especially in the semi-final against Pakistan, Dhoni managed to hold the side together well even in the face of extreme provocation of the high-pitched nature of the contest. Then in Mumbai during the final at the Wankhede Stadium, Dhoni was probably the one man who did not show much pressure.

The way he batted in a high-pressure chase was noteworthy. He did not flinch even once and got himself promoted ahead of an in-form Yuvraj Singh. The way Gautam Gambhir and he turned the tide will forever be etched in every Indian's mind.

The whole country celebrated and the time it took for us to reach our homes that night was testimony to the impact of the triumph. But I felt that night a lot of things changed around Indian cricket. I mean not just about Dhoni going bald.

It was in many ways the end of an era, because there seemed to be a complete lack of respect for the way Test cricket needed to be played. The emphasis was on the fact that we are the world champions. But everyone forgot that it was just in the one-day format. India seemed to slip further down the radar in the Test format. The 2011 England tour was one of the worst in recent times in Indian Test history. I have not seen a more abject surrender than on that tour. I would pin the blame on captain Dhoni.

The Indian side was disjointed, injured and disappointed a number of fans. The players seemed to have gone a bit easy after winning the World Cup. The fire was missing in the belly in some of the players and Test cricket seemed a format that they did not wish to be part of, it seemed. At some level the attitude also showed in the way Dhoni handled the losses, at least in the press conferences. The English tour was followed by another disaster in Australia and another 0-4 whitewash. Again the skipper spoke about how the 2007 World Cup exit was a bigger disaster. That was enough to set the alarm bells ringing at least in the traditional fans of the game in India.

I cannot for a moment imagine any other Indian captain surviving such disastrous results. But Dhoni survived only because of the fact that he seemed to have support of the right people in the right places. Then, Dhoni started losing great players like Dravid, VVS Laxman among others. The other players like Virender Sehwag, Zaheer Khan and Harbhajan Singh started under-performing. It was generally a period of flux for Indian cricket, yet again.

To make matters worse no one seemed to want to address the Tendulkar question. Finally, even the great man pulled the plug on his career. Dhoni did manage to inflict a 4-0 series defeat on a divided touring Australian squad in 2012–13. But the Test drive was clearly missing in Dhoni.

The entire Test squad was recast with a number of young players like Virat Kohli, Ajinkya Rahane, Cheteshwar Pujara and Mohammed Shami making the starting XI. With a new squad in tow, Dhoni seemed to have rediscovered some mojo in the Test format in South Africa and New Zealand. There were opportunities which India needed to have captured, but let go of because of some timid captaincy.

I was disappointed with the way Dhoni led on the two tours. I felt the end was nigh for Dhoni in the Test match format. He was not one to brood over reaching the 100 Test match target. He managed to add the Champions Trophy title in 2013, so the legend of Dhoni as ODI captain grew further. The crown in the T20I format seemed to be far away from him and the team's radar.

But the most disappointing aspect of Dhoni's end as a Test cricketer was the way he called it quits. In the middle of a tough away Test series, Dhoni called it quits just after he finished a press conference, where he gave no indication of his impending retirement. It did not sit well with me, but the call had been made.

Dhoni just wanted to concentrate on the ODI and T20I formats. That was a fair call. In my view Dhoni should have quit Test captaincy at the end of the 2011–12 season when India had managed to end with disastrous results. If Dhoni had quit the format or the captaincy, India would have been better served. But the fact that he delayed his retirement or resignation meant that India lost out on rebuilding the Test side. Virat Kohli had been further delayed in building a side that can take on the world.

The World Cup in 2015 was the best chance for Dhoni to redeem some pride for India. But India failed to dislodge the host Australia from the post of eminence and let go of a golden chance to win the title twice in a row. But Dhoni was already under a lot of pressure at home. The way he was subjected to scrutiny owing to the scandals in the Indian Premier League (IPL) broke my heart. Just how a legend like Dhoni could let himself be subjected to such a searching examination is beyond me.

Dhoni, much like the other legends of Indian cricket kept quiet in the face of extreme crisis and let me, a fan of this game, down. I would have expected a bit more of an honest and open approach to this menace of corruption in the sport. Instead, if reports are right Dhoni did not add to the investigation in a big way. I was disappointed with the outcome. Dhoni has been and will always be a huge hero for Indians and for me particularly. I think all the goodwill that Dhoni gained over the years has been squandered by this IPL fiasco.

I hope in the future we do get to hear from the great man on what he thought actually happened.

Also I hope someday he is able to come clean on the way seniors like VVS Laxman and Virender Sehwag, among others ended their careers abruptly. They did not really have good things to say about the way their careers ended. Even the likes of Yuvraj Singh, Harbhajan Singh and Gautam Gambhir were dumped unceremoniously. There seemed to be no communication and that reflected poorly in the way Dhoni handled the side.

Let's hope for the sake of future Indian cricketers, there is better communication. Hopefully, Dhoni will lead the way in ensuring the same. We do not know how much longer Dhoni will play for India.

But barring the last half of his career, Dhoni has been in an unique position to view the changing equations of Indian cricket from close quarters, since he has played with three generations of Indian cricketers.

Let's hope someday he does reveal it all and thereby regains fans like me.

***

Lessons Learnt

There is a lot to learn from this league of extraordinary gentlemen. They make such fine ambassadors of this great country of ours.

While picking these 10 cricketers I did not have to think much because each of these gentlemen have made an impact on our lives in the last 25 years.

Whether it is the Fabulous Four of Sachin Tendulkar, Rahul Dravid, Sourav Ganguly and VVS Laxman, or the spin duo of Anil Kumble and Harbhajan Singh, fantastic Virender Sehwag, flamboyant Yuvraj or the ever cool Mahendra Singh Dhoni or the magical Zaheer Khan, they have all made an impact in different ways.

I have a lot to learn from each of these gentlemen because they have different qualities. Tendulkar's humility is a lesson for all of us, Dravid's steely resolve is worth emulating, Ganguly and MS Dhoni offer contrasting lessons in leadership skills. Similarly the fighting spirit of the spin pair of Kumble and Harbhajan or the devil-may-care attitude of Sehwag or the sheer natural ability of Yuvraj, coupled with the self-confidence of Zaheer. All this has impacted me and no doubt billions of others.

As I compiled this book, I was left wondering how wonderful it was for Indian cricket to have all these gentlemen play almost at the same time. Very rarely have cricket teams been built around individuals who are the best at what they do. It is indeed a privilege and a honour to have seen these extraordinary cricketers in the same era. One can learn so much from simply playing back their exploits. The videos of their efforts still make for compelling viewing.

As you would imagine I am a complete cricket nut. For me nothing else mattered. It therefore felt great to compile my thoughts on these 10 extraordinary cricketers.

***

About the Author

Kapil Pathare
(Director - Maxwell Industries Ltd.)

At the start of the 21st century, Maxwell Industries Ltd., a VIP Group Company, witnessed the introduction of an enthusiastic, young and dynamic leader in the Board of Directors.

Kapil Jaykumar Pathare engraved his name in the company at the tender age of 21, and impressed the whole company with his situational leadership style, spot decision-making abilities and as an effective communicator of management decisions. Since the beginning, he has been inclined towards the operations side. He focussed more on various aspects of manufacturing of innerwear with a clear concept of quality of products and services. He always describes Maxwell as a pioneer of innerwear manufacturers and an innovating marketing company. With this enthusiasm and customer oriented global vision, he has made great changes in the manufacturing and marketing traditions and styles. He possesses an absolutely clear vision to make the brand a global success. He believes the company's success depends on the right understanding of human resources, and the skills and values of those who work in the organisation.

Kapil pursued his Masters in Business Administration after his graduation in Commerce, and has equipped himself on the professional front by attending various seminars, conferences and updating himself through the mentoring process.

The company has been continuously engaged in branding of products and enhancing its image from a mass brand to a premium brand. The company's foresight in placing Frenchie and Frenchie X innerwear brands in the Indian market and abroad have created a passion for innerwear in India's young generation.

He is also in-charge of the other business owned by the family like Jet Klean Laundry, Shogun Chemicals Pvt. Ltd., Pathare Dairy and Agriculture.

He also heads Maxwell Entertainment Pvt Ltd., a strategic tie-up with event companies for organising various cultural, film, and biking events. His passion for riding bikes brings him satisfaction in life. Kapil is a true cricket lover and loves watching the game at stadiums, and even travels to different parts of world to do so.

His first book *Cricket to Corporate* (2014) was launched by ex-wicket keeper Kiran More who said, "Cricket is not just a game, but a field where corporate strategies are planned and executed live."

***